The Texture of Truth

By the same author:

> Divine Redemption and the Refuge of Faith
> Christian Confession and the Crackling Thorn: The Imperatives of Faith in an Age of Unbelief
> The Fracture of Faith: Recovering Belief of the Gospel in a Postmodern World
> The Bondage of Grace
> Man in the Maelstrom of Modern Thought: An Essay in Theological Perspective
> Now That You Have Believed: An Exploration of the Life and Walk of Faith
> Christian Truth in Critical Times
> Studies in the Theory of Money 1690-1776
> A Study of Mutual Funds (with Irwin Friend, F. E. Brown, and Edward S. Herman)
> The Theory of the Firm: Production, Capital, and Finance
> Financial Markets in the Capitalist Process
> Economics and Man
> A Christian Approach to Economics and the Cultural Condition
> Money Capital in the Theory of the Firm
> Money, Banking, and the Macroeconomy
> Economics and the Antagonism of Time: Time, Uncertainty, and Choice in Economic Theory
> The Tyranny of the Market: A Critique of Theoretical Foundations
> Economics and Ethics: An Introduction to Theory, Institutions, and Policy

The Texture of Truth

Essential theology
in the life and walk of faith

Douglas Vickers

REFORMATION HERITAGE BOOKS
Grand Rapids, Michigan

Copyright © 2007
Douglas Vickers

Published by
Reformation Heritage Books
2965 Leonard St., NE
Grand Rapids, MI 49525
616-977-0599 / Fax 616-285-3246
e-mail: orders@heritagebooks.org
website: www.heritagebooks.org

ISBN 978-1-60178-009-6

All rights reserved.

For additional Reformed literature, both new and used, request a free book list from the above address.

Preface

The thought-forms and the behavior-norms of the world press with uncommon clamor on the Christian and the church in this time. But in the context in which the church takes its place in the world the generality of Christian profession is not marked and protected by a high degree of doctrinal self-consciousness. Too easily, a less than adequately informed profession tarnishes the meaning of Christian commitment, the grounds of belief are vague and held with unnecessary insecurity, and a tenuous hold on truth diminishes the health and vitality of the Christian's life. I have accordingly endeavored in this brief work to call attention to a number of basic doctrines that form a nexus of what I have called "essential theology in the life and walk of faith." I have in no sense intended or attempted to present a systematic theology. But I have written with the conviction that nothing is more productive of sound Christian experience, and nothing points more securely to the progress in sanctification to which the Christian is called, than Christian doctrine soundly understood, held in biblical proportion, and soundly applied.

The objectives I have held in view have caused me to avoid excessive footnotes that might detract by giving the impression of a primarily academic interest. In the following chapters I have tried to maintain the focus of discussion on the relevance of biblical doctrine for a basic understanding of the Christian faith and its biblical expression. My objective is to bring to clear perspective the meaning and the progress of the Christian life. The cardinal doctrines I address are those prominent in a commitment to the Reformed tradition in theology: The doctrines of God, Scripture, the divine Covenants, Creation and the Fall, Christ's redemptive offices, the application of redemption, and the place of the Christian in the church and in the world.

My indebtedness to the long line of Reformed theologians, some of whom are acknowledged at the outset, will be clear to the informed reader. We stand in this day on the shoulders of better scholars who have preceded us. I acknowledge cheerfully also the assistance of a number of people. I am indebted to Dr. Joel Beeke for valuable editorial suggestions and to Jay Collier and the staff of Reformation Heritage Books for their detailed work leading to publication; discussions in the adult Sunday School class it has been my privilege to lead for some years have sharpened my theological perceptions; Ann Hopkins assisted me in preparing the manuscript for the press. My prayer is that the argument I have presented will be of value to those into whose hands we must soon, under the guidance of the purpose and providence of God, leave the future of the church and its testimony. I reserve to myself responsibility for the blemishes that remain in the work.

Contents

Preface — v

1. The Nature and Scope of Christian Doctrine — 1
2. God, His Being and Attributes — 21
3. The Biblical Revelation and the Knowledge of God — 44
4. The Covenant-making God — 63
5. Man, Created and Fallen — 83
6. The Person of Christ — 106
7. The Redemptive Office Of Christ — 122
8. The Application of Redemption: Regeneration, Justification, Sanctification — 144
9. The Christian in the Church and in the World — 170

Index of Scripture References — 191
Index of Subjects and Names — 197

Chapter 1

The Nature and Scope of Christian Doctrine

Theology, once regarded among the learned disciplines as the queen of the sciences, has fallen on hard times. Philosophers have bowed in obeisance to its agenda, churchmen have wrestled with its demanding scope, and by its demands and perspectives Christian confessors have determined their life-form and belief. But the golden age of theology has passed. Lesser preoccupations and arguments grounded in shallower presuppositions have taken its place. The "God-question," as it came to be called, the question of the existence, the being, and the purposes of God, no longer has a meaningful place in the intellectual scheme of things. The system-builders in philosophy have given way to a blunt and agnostic atheism. Modernism and the assumed competence and autonomy of reason has turned into a postmodernism in which truth has been diminished to truths, where everyman's truth is as good as another's, and absolute criteria of belief and behavior no longer exist. The world of thought has conceded predominance to a man-centered materialism, and opinion-formers in the church have capitulated to cultural accommodation and depreciated doctrine. The Christian believer has been left to Milton's lament: "The hungry sheep look up, and are not fed." "Blind mouths," Milton characterized the pastors of the church, "that scarce themselves know how to hold a sheep-hook."[1] The indictment presses with a new urgency in our time. Its relevance and terms could be expanded.

The church, of course, has been blessed by large and important theologies. It is not our intention to reproduce or challenge or replace them. Calvin, Turretin, Witsius, and their Reformed successors in the sixteenth and seventeenth centuries in continental Europe; Owen, Goodwin, Howe and the host of Puritan theologians in seventeenth-century England; Edwards in America in the eighteenth century; the Scottish masters, Chalmers, Cunningham, Smeaton in the nineteenth century; Bavinck in Holland and Alexander, Hodge, Warfield, Dabney, and Thornwell in nineteenth-century America; and their successors, Vos, Machen, Murray, Van Til and their colleagues, along with Berkhof and Reymond, in the twentieth century – the list of distinctively Reformed theologians embarrasses by the need to abbreviate and leave worthy names unsung. But in our own time theology is at a discount among confessing Christian believers. The seminary study is often trapped in a capitulation to contemporary philosophic thought-forms that trickle their damaging descent to the pulpit, or it is distant from the pew and from the worshipers worried by the state of their soul.

The following chapters do not set out to present a systematic theology. The end in view, rather, is that of presenting for calm consideration a number of principal issues and themes from biblical theology. The issues and questions chosen for review should bear with immediate urgency on the understanding, commitment, and life of the Christian in the

---

[1] John Milton, *Lycidas*, lines 125 and 119-20, in M. H. Abrams, et al., eds., *The Norton Anthology of English Literature* (New York: Norton, 1962).

hurrying pressures of everyday. That objective means that the issues we address and the areas of biblical doctrine we consider will necessarily be highly selective. The intention is to open for wider examination and thought a number of basic and essential doctrines of Christian belief that will contribute to a sounder progress in Christian understanding and life. We begin with some preliminary definitions and questions that will set the stage for what follows.

Some preliminary definitions

First, what is to be understood by the word or the concept "doctrine" that we shall use extensively? In brief terms, a *doctrine* is an ordered statement of what is believed in an area of knowledge or understanding or in the explanation of a part or aspect of life and reality. What we hold as doctrine, as Christian doctrine for example, is related to what is frequently referred to as the *dogma* of the church. By that latter term we mean the statements of faith that have been accorded formal agreement by the councils of the church and have become part of the systematized body of belief and testimony to which the church is formally committed. In that sense, the doctrines to which we hold, communicated in the revelation that God has made, have been consolidated in various ways in the historic confessions of the church. Some of those confessional statements will engage us again. But it is already implicit in what has been said that our concern is not simply with doctrine in a formal and undelineated sense. Our concern is with *Christian doctrine*, and what is contemplated under that head can be stated as follows.

Christian doctrine is an ordered system of belief regarding (i) the being of God, his essence, triune existence, attributes, decrees, purposes, and works, and (ii) the state of mankind in relation to God, and, in the light of man's fallen condition in sin, the provision for his redemption and the prospects for his eternal destiny and security. It will follow that the ultimate locus of Christian doctrine, or the source from which the terms and limits of doctrine derive, is the inscripturated revelation that has been given and preserved for our guidance. The locus of doctrinal authority and the criteria of correctness and validity of doctrine are found in the Scriptures. Their canonical authority culminated in the church's reception of the apostolic literature, and the canon was closed with the termination of the apostolic age. In the Scriptures, informing as they do all that is to be said in the discussion of Christian doctrine, God has said his last word to man. God has nothing to say to man that he has not already said. Progressive illumination and deepening understanding of the word from God necessarily occur. But as to the inspired revelation as such, its content was definitively determined and was terminated with the close of the biblical canon. The Scriptures as given are thus the final, inspired, inerrant, sufficient, and authoritative word to us.

Our tour of the theological terrain will bring us into contact with two terms, *religion* and *theology*, the meanings of which need to be distinguished. By *religion* we mean essentially our relation to God and what follows from it regarding our conduct and character or the way we order our lives. We shall see that an inevitability, with its influence and implications for conduct and behavior, attaches to the religious dimension of life. That fact has deep and widening significance for all that will be said in what follows. For it is to be held as a basic and foundational proposition, a presupposition that determines all subsequent flow of thought, that we exist because we have been created as the image of God. We say that by virtue of his creation man is the image of God. We can make that statement in more precise terms. We say, not that man in some sense *bears* the image of God. We maintain on the grounds of the explanatory revelation of the Scriptures that man *is* the image of God. We say that man *is* the image of God in that he is created, soul and body, male and female, an immortal, rational, spiritual, moral, and speaking person, capable of reflective self-awareness and purposive action, characterized in his created condition by knowledge and by constitutive holiness and righteousness, and endowed with the capacity for the reception of divine revelation, social relations and communication, and communion with God his Creator. That statement of man's created condition and constitution, with the recognition of the high status and privileges that follow from it, points to the meaning and significance of religion as consisting essentially in one's relation to God.

The estate in which our first parents were established and came to self-consciousness was surrendered by their fall into sin. The result of that Fall, the outcome of Adam's failure to adhere to the terms of probation that God had communicated to him, was to cast into the state of sin all those who have descended from him by ordinary generation. The fact that our first parents repudiated their covenantal obligations has meant that "in Adam all die" (1 Cor. 15:22), and that "by one man's [Adam's] disobedience many were made sinners" (Rom. 5:19). For "as by one man sin entered the world, and death by sin ... so death passed upon all men, for that all have sinned" (Rom. 5:12). When Adam fell, we all fell. That is the meaning of the imputation to us of the guilt of Adam's first sin. As the Westminster Shorter Catechism states it, "The covenant being made with Adam, not only for himself, but for his posterity; all mankind, descending from him, by ordinary generation, sinned in him, and fell with him, in his first transgression."[2] Adam was a public person, the fruits of whose dereliction from the covenant of creation descend to us all.

From the meaning of the created order of human affairs it follows that man is a religious being. He is a religious being because he is the image of God. That is how he must be primarily and principally understood. We shall return to further implications of the fact. But for the present we take note of one principal point of significance. If it is to be seen

---

[2] Westminster Shorter Catechism, Question 16.

that man is essentially a religious being, then it follows that all that he is and does will be influenced and determined by his religious orientation and commitment. It will depend on and will be consistent with the nature, the direction, and the quality of his religion and the life-structure and behavior it determines. That statement can be expanded for our present purposes to say that man will, as a result, necessarily hold to either a godly or a godless religion. The religious characterization of his being and personhood will necessarily come to expression in his worshiping the true God or his worshiping an idol. From that it follows that his entire culture will be influenced and determined by either a godly or a godless religion, and it will become what it is because of its grounding in that religious formation. In that ultimate and residual respect, culture is a part of religion, in the sense that the nature and intrinsic quality of culture will be determined by the religion, godly or godless, from which it derives and by which it is informed.

The final term we have referred to is *theology*. Its relation to *religion* is to be held in mind. *Theology* (or, in our present concern, theological doctrine) is the formulated system of belief that comes from the study of what God has revealed and which explains our relation to him. Religion and theology are thus both responses to God's revelation. Theology studies and systematizes what God has revealed. Religion is concerned with our living out before God the implications of that revelation. Theology, therefore, is a human enterprise. Reflecting again on man's created rationality, and recognizing the need it implies to organize systematically what we know, we will necessarily systematize our knowledge and comprehension of the revelation of God into an ordered and more or less systematic whole. The systematized knowledge statement that we have thus constructed is what we mean by theology. It will follow that such a systematized understanding, or one's *theology*, may or may not be true to, in the sense that it is consistent with, what the Scriptures contain and have declared. Theology may be a consistently biblical theology, or it may be in various ways and to a greater or lesser extent errant or heretical theology.

Why study Christian doctrine?

Why is the study of Christian doctrine necessary, and what motivates a study of its ethical imperatives in what is frequently characterized as a post-Christian age? For what significance does Christian doctrine assume in an age when rational judgment has rejected the possibility that theological or any other absolutes exist, and when moral relativism has substantially captured the soul? A first answer to the question is contained implicitly in what has been said. The very motivation to understand and systematize the knowledge of what our faith and belief depend upon is innate to the rationality inherent in our personhood. But beyond that, and beyond all the relevant demands and proclivities to systematic understanding, compelling reasons exist why the Christian believer, if he or she is to live a healthy Christian life in the pursuit of holiness and the knowledge of God, will want to understand the doctrinal content of the faith. For what we have already said means that doctrine determines life. We are what we believe. Being is prior to doing. It would seem on the very surface of things that the reasons for the study of doctrine include: the need to understand in whatever depth is possible our personal relation to God; the need to understand our place in the church; and the need to understand the respects in which the Christian's walk in this world should be consistent with the status of redemption in Christ to which, by the grace of God, he has been raised.

The knowledge of God and his redemptive purposes

"Why study Christian doctrine?" Two immediate reasons reside in what it is that determines the Christian's situation:

first, the realization of the state of sin to which we were reduced by Adam's Fall; and second, the status to which we have been raised by virtue of our redemption by Christ and our union with him. The Christian believer is a person who has been transferred, as the theologian John Murray put it, from the realm of "sin-condemnation-death" to that of "righteousness-justification-life."[3] What, then, is the meaning of the Christian life that follows as a result? In what respects, and why, does it differ from life in the world? What are the imperatives for conduct it contains? And what is the prospect it projects for eternal felicity and security?

More extended answers to these questions will engage us in due course. But to comment briefly at this point on what is involved, consider the matter of one's relation to God. We have put the Christian's personal knowledge of God and his purpose first among the reasons for studying Christian doctrine. The very question whether God exists has been at times the hunting ground of the philosophers and opinion-formers in the history of thought. Various so-called proofs of God's existence have been proposed. Thomas Aquinas, the systematizing philosopher-theologian of the thirteenth century, became justly famous for his arguments in that direction. The details need not detain us. But comparable arguments – the so-called ontological, cosmological, moral, and teleological proofs (based, respectively, on the supposition that if a perfect being can be contemplated in thought then he or it must exist; the argument that a first cause must exist; the claim that a god must exist to administer justice in another world; the proposition that a purpose must exist to explain all things) – these arguments have found currency in the learned literature down to the present day. Immanuel Kant, the philosopher who flourished at the culmination of the eighteenth-century Enlightenment, is famous for, among other

---

[3] John Murray, *The Epistle to the Romans* (Grand Rapids: Eerdmans, 1959), vol. 1, 179.

things, the argument that the "proofs" are fallacious; and he consigned God to a realm (his "noumenal realm") in which and about which knowledge was impossible. But we are interested at the moment in a much more important question.

For us, the statement that *God is* is our basic apologetic presupposition. And what we are addressing at present is not the possibility *that* God is, or that he is not. For even Kant agreed that while it was impossible to prove that God existed, it was equally impossible to prove that he did not exist. We are concerned with the question of *who* God is and what are the attributes of his being that make the character of his essence knowable to us. Our proposition, therefore, is that the first reason for the Christian's interest in Christian doctrine is that he or she might thereby know more clearly and fully who God is and what are the possibilities of our relation with him.

The apostle John has recorded the statement of our Lord in his High Priestly prayer that "This is life eternal, that they might know thee the only true God, and Jesus Christ, whom thou hast sent" (John 17:3). But what, it is necessary to ask, are the grounds on which the knowledge of God is possible? What, it follows, has God done in the implementation of his redemptive purpose to make it possible that sinners who were by nature at enmity against him could again be reconciled to him and know him? What transaction occurred within the eternal council of the Godhead, in which redemptive offices were assumed by the Father, the Son, and the Holy Spirit, that instigated and brought to completion the process of redemption? And what, as a result, followed as the work in this world of the second Person of the Godhead who became Jesus Christ for our redemption? The questions multiply when we begin to examine the doctrinal content of what has been revealed in those respects.

But we bring to pointed emphasis why the study of Christian doctrine finds its first answer in the possibility and necessity of the knowledge of God. The knowledge of God and his redemptive purpose projects its significance to the very core of meaning of the Christian life. It carries with it the conviction that the Holy Spirit, whom Christ has sent, will apply to the people he redeemed the benefits of that redemption, and that the Holy Spirit will infallibly conduct those people to glory. The doctrine of the assured destiny of the saints is extensively displayed on the pages of Scripture. If that is so, then the assured prospect is held before the Christian that "when he [Christ] shall appear, we shall be like him" (1 John 3:2); and that the believer will come at last to "the measure of the stature of the fullness of Christ" (Eph. 4:13). "When Christ, who is our life, shall appear, then shall ye also appear with him in glory" (Col. 3:4). The conviction follows in the Christian consciousness that an imperative is implied for his conduct and life in this world. Laid upon the Christian conscience is the necessity of progress in sanctification and holiness, "without which," as the letter to the Hebrews stated it, "no man shall see the Lord" (Heb. 12:14).

Coming to focus in these ways are the doctrines that constitute the very groundwork of Christian belief. They explain the ground of our justification, the counsel and covenantal purpose of God that was implemented in the process of redemption, the Person and work of Christ who came as our substitute redeemer, and the application by the Holy Spirit of the redemption that he accomplished. The response is elicited from the Christian that the pursuit of sanctification is the demanding imperative of his life. It is the understanding of the doctrinal nexus and the explanatory statements of the Scriptures on these points that answer on this first level why the study of Christian doctrine is necessary.

The Christian's place in the church

The study of Christian doctrine is necessary, we said in the second place, because by virtue of his commitment to Christ the Christian believer is joined in an organic union to the church that Christ redeemed. The doctrine of the church looms large in the Christian believer's consciousness. It has been anticipated in what has been said that the eternal covenant of redemption between the Persons of the Godhead means and implies that Christ redeemed the people whom God the Father gave to him before the foundation of the world. "Thine they were," Christ prays to the Father, "and thou gavest them me" (John 17:6). They were the sheep for whom the shepherd died. He knew their names and to them he gives eternal life (John 10:3, 11, 14, 15, 28). It was the church for which Christ died, for those, in their unique identity and particularity, whose sins he bore. He "loved the church," the apostle explained to the Ephesians, "and gave himself for it" (Eph. 5:24). And for that reason the apostle charged the elders of the Ephesian church to "feed the church of God, which he hath purchased with his own blood" (Acts 20:28). The resulting fact and the doctrine of the believer's union with Christ make their pressing demands on the Christian's understanding and belief.

The Christian is an eschatological person. He is one whose life in this world is consonant with the expectation that he will share with his Lord in the last great day the eternal reign of glory, the inheritance to which, by the grace of God, he is destined. The promise of eternal inheritance steels his nerve and strengthens his soul in this life as he assents to the summary statement of the letter to the Hebrews: "For this cause he [Christ] is the mediator of the new testament, that by means of death, for the redemption of the transgressions that were under the first testament, they which are called might receive the promise of eternal inheritance [or the eternal inheritance that has been promised]" (Heb. 9:15). By virtue of his completed redemptive work Christ has been established "Heir of all things" (Heb. 1:2), and he has called his people to share that inheritance with him.

The Christian knows that it was the guilt of his particular sin for which Christ died. It was the grace of the Spirit of God to him personally and individually that conveyed to him the gifts of repentance and faith and that turned his steps to see Christ as the Savior of sinners. We are brought to Christ one by one. Christ has set his favor on each of his people individually. But the individualness of salvation, the fact that each believer in his own particularity is brought by grace to the kingdom of Christ, carries with it a new awareness and conviction. That rests in the understanding, born with clarity from the scriptural testimony, that he is rescued from the estate of sin because he was numbered among the church that God gave to his Son to redeem. It is as a part of the church that the believer is redeemed. It is therefore into the church, the organic entity that was the subject of God's eternal decree to redeem, that the Christian is incorporated.

The doctrine of the church opens its meaning for the Christian believer on a number of levels: first, the explanation of the decrees of God that predestined the church, and the subject members of the church in their individuality and particularity, to redemption and eternal security in Christ; second, the distinctions and the relations between the church in its invisible and its visible aspects; third, the manner in which the Scriptures have established what is required of the organization, the government, and the forms of worship of the church visible (the church as it exists in a corporate form in this world – sometimes referred to as the church militant as distinct from the church triumphant); and fourth, the necessary conduct of the members of the church in their relations within the particular culture into which they are admitted, as distinct from the culture of the world from which they have been brought by the grace of God.

The Christian's place in the church expands its significance to the correct understanding of the privileges and responsibilities it conveys. Though we are brought into the church one by one, as individuals responsible for our personal acts of repentance and faith in Christ, we do not live and behave in the church individualistically. Brought as we are to an organic union with Christ, incorporated into the organic entity of the church, we participate in an assured hope, an eschatological prospect, that has an organic dimension. The Christian's hope is not only or simply his hope and prospect of personal perseverance. At issue also is the prospect he holds of the eschatological condition and the eternal preservation of the church into the membership of which he has been incorporated. That means that the Christian's life in this world will be determined as to its character by the culture of faith that membership of the church connotes. The Scriptures are eloquent in clarifying the privileges and responsibilities of membership of the community of saints that constitute the church. The relevant doctrines will engage the believer's careful attention. The first epistle of John, for example, presents many aspects of the mutual love and affection of the saints that receive ready assent from the true believer. The distinctiveness of the church lies in the common doctrine it professes and in the mutual love of its members of which John has spoken.

The Christian's life in the world

Our third reason for the study of Christian doctrine is that it throws its light on the Christian's life and conduct in relation to the world. At a minimum, the Christian's life should be consistent with the status he now enjoys as one who has been redeemed by Christ. Biblical doctrine addresses a threefold aspect of what is involved.

First, it makes the negative point that the Christian believer no longer belongs to the world. For consider the state and condition from which he or she has been transferred into the kingdom of Christ. The Jews on one occasion remonstrated with our Lord when he said that belief in him would free them from the bondage in which they were held. If you "know the truth ... the truth shall make you free." "We be Abraham's seed," the Jews responded, "and were never in bondage to any man" (John 10:32-33). But Christ went on to insist that the bondage of which he spoke was the bondage to sin. "Whosoever committeth sin is the servant [the slave] of sin" (John 10:34). He made the same point on another momentous occasion when he said by analogy that "When a strong man armed keepeth his palace, his goods are in peace. But when a stronger than he shall come upon him, and overcome him, he taketh from him all his armour wherein he trusted" (Luke 11:21-22). The "strong man armed," the devil, keeps the unregenerate person in a slumber of sin. That is why it is said that Christ came "that he might destroy the works of the devil" (1 John 3:8), and that "through death he might destroy him that had the power of death, that is, the devil" (Heb. 2:14). It is from such a state of enslavement to sin that the Christian has been "delivered from the power of darkness, and ... translated into the kingdom of his [God's] dear Son" (Col. 1:13). The scriptural explanation could be expanded.

By the reference to the world in this context is meant the thought-forms, the allegiances, the meaning-systems, the behavioral principles, and the entire belief and ethical constructs that characterize the culture of the world apart from God. Whereas the Christian was at one time in subjugation to all that is involved in such a godless culture and alliance, his redemption and his coming to faith in Christ mean that now he has been translated to a completely different and antithetical realm. We put that previously by saying that the believer in Christ has been transferred from the realm of sin, condemnation, and death to that of righteousness, justification, and life. The Christian, then, no longer belongs to the world. The apostle Paul made the same point in his letter to the Ephesians, speaking to the Gentiles of their new condition and privileges. Paul made the sixfold point: the Gentiles had been (i) "without Christ;" (ii) "aliens from the commonwealth of Israel;" (iii) "strangers from the covenants of promise;" (iv) "having no hope;" (v) "without God;" and (vi) "in the world" (Eph. 2:12). The climax of the apostle's statement is that those without Christ were "in the world." It is on grounds such as those that we say that the Christian now is no longer in the world. He has been introduced to a new, a different, an antithetical realm and culture.

Second, the Christian, whose aim is to exhibit in his life-commitment what follows from and is implied by his participation in the culture of the church, no longer aligns his life with what we have just seen life in the world to entail. Because the Christian belongs to a different culture, the scriptural doctrine is expansive on the obligation and privilege he enjoys of being a light in the world, to work by his confession as salt in whatever unsavory context he finds himself, and to witness to the truth as it is in Christ Jesus. The Christian is in the world, but he does not belong to the world. It is true that because the world hated the Son of God when he came, and because even "his own received him not" (John 1:11), the world will in turn hate those who belong to him. The reality should be confronted in the spirit of realism with which our Lord himself spoke: "If the world hate you, ye know that it hated me before it hated you. If ye were of the world, the world would love his own; but because ye are not of the world, but I have chosen you out of the world, therefore the world hateth you" (John 15:18-19). But the realism involved in that condition does not call for a hatred on the part of the Christian for those who are still "in the world." It is the world-system as we have already connoted it that is the subject of the Christian's rejection. The apostle John has made the distinction clear in his summing up: "Love not the world, neither the things that are in the world. If any man love the world, the love of the Father is not in him. For all that is in the world, the lust of the flesh, and the lust of the eyes, and the pride of life, is not of the Father, but is of the world. And the world passeth away, and the lust thereof; but he that doeth the will of God abideth for ever" (1 John 2:15-17).

Because the Christian understands and lives in the light of what God has done in calling him into the kingdom of Christ, he will follow the scriptural injunctions as to how he should live in the world until the day of his eternal inheritance. The sovereign and eternal purposes of God in calling to himself his people whom Christ redeemed will be fulfilled in the ways of God's appointment. And in the working out of those sovereign designs, the Christian confession and the Christian confessors remain in the world to announce the mercy of God in Christ. They are to be the instruments of grace in bringing God's intentions of mercy to their culmination.

That means that the objective of the Christian's testimony to the world is to invite men into the kingdom of Christ. We know that Christ did not make an indiscriminate atonement, in that he did not die to bear the sins of all men indiscriminately. He died, as we have already seen, for those whom the Father gave him to redeem before the foundation of the world. But the mandate to the church and to the Christian is that the announcement must be made indiscriminately that salvation is freely available in Christ to all who will believe. For our Lord himself has said that "him that cometh to me I will in no wise cast out" (John 6:37). And the gospel declaration rings with undiminished clarity that whosoever will may be saved. It is the Christian's privilege and task to make that declaration with sincerity and compassion to all who will hear.

The Scriptures are eloquent in the consistent declaration that the atonement that Christ made was a particular atonement. He died to save particular people. For that reason Christ prefaced the statement we have just adduced by saying that "All that the Father giveth me shall come to me" (John 6:37). God's purposes in redemption will be unfailingly accomplished and all those whom Christ redeemed by his life and death in this world will be saved. The gospel invitation is in the meantime spread by the church to all people everywhere. Whosoever will may come in faith to Christ. But, it may be asked, "Who will come?" The answer is insistent in the Word of God, in the same manner as we have just seen it in the statement of Christ, that those will come whom the Father calls by the effectual call of the Holy Spirit. In his same discourse on his identity as the bread of life Christ stated that "No man can come unto me, except the Father which hath sent me draw him" (John 6:44). And "Every man that hath heard, and hath learned of [or from] the Father cometh unto me" (John 6:45).

The church and the Christian witness exist, then, to call those who are still "in the world" to come into the church. We put the statement in that form because, as we have seen, it is the church, the organic entity of the kingdom of Christ, into which the believer in Christ has been incorporated. But in making that witness and sounding that call, it is to be realized that the hearers will be interested in coming into the church, not because the church and the people of the church have in one way or another made themselves like the world, but because the world sees that the church is different. It must be the attraction of a different culture, the attraction of the difference of the life that is committed to Christ, that will be relevant. In making its call, therefore, the Christian testimony will not be presented in a manner that makes concession to the thought-patterns and the behavior-patterns of the world. The culture of the church is a different culture. Its difference from the idioms of the world is to be guarded and preserved. The scriptural doctrine on the point is inescapable.

The third respect in which Christian doctrine is relevant to the Christian's life in the world can be referred to briefly at this point. It has to do with the important question of how, when, and in what way the church can and should make a contribution to social, political, or economic discourse and affairs. The extent of the church's prerogative in these respects has been variously understood, but in short, the following can be said by way of immediate guidance.

The mandate of the church, as Paul said to Timothy, is to "preach the word" (2 Tim. 4:2). In that, he was defining the principal and the only duty and responsibility of the church. Whatever else the church does is to be done in the context of its preaching the Word and is to be consistent with it. That essential focus of the church's mandate precludes it from participating directly in matters of governmental, industrial, or political policy, in relation to which there is no reason to believe the church has any competence. In that respect a distinction is to be drawn between the prerogatives and responsibilities of the church as the church, and those of Christian men as Christian men. It is the privilege of the latter to bring to bear on their sphere of influence the imperatives of the Christian faith as they are relevant to questions of social and political interest. But specific policy issues and questions are beyond the mandate of the church as the church, except as comment on them can be shown to be necessary by reason of their relation to, and their conceivable transgressions of, the moral law.

We have considered the question, "Why study Christian doctrine?" and have suggested that at a minimum the answer has to do with (i) the need to know God and understand the possibility and potentialities of life in communion with him; (ii) the need to understand the Christian's place in the church; and (iii) the need to hold a clear view of the place and responsibility of the Christian in the world. We can now take note in a similarly introductory way of the principal areas of Christian doctrine that will engage us more fully.

The scope of Christian doctrine

Our study in the following chapters will focus on five of the principal areas of Christian doctrine: (i) the doctrine of God and his covenantal purpose and relations with man whom he created in his own image; (ii) the doctrine of man, including his creation and his fall in Adam from his covenantal obligations and the implications of that fall for all those descending from our first parents by ordinary generation; (iii) the doctrine of the Person and work of Christ, and the rescue from the entailment of sin of those he came to save; (iv) the doctrine of the Person and work of the Holy Spirit in the application to those whom Christ redeemed of the benefits of the redemption he accomplished; and (v) the doctrine of the church.

One final preliminary point is to be borne in mind. Biblical theology is covenantal theology. It is for that reason we have said that the doctrine of God takes up the doctrine of his covenantal purpose. All of God's dealings with man are in one way or another covenantal. The implications will be pervasive in what follows. In his initial created state, Adam's relation to his Creator-God was what it was because God established a covenant with him. That is variously referred to as the covenant of works or the covenant of creation. It contained within its terms the promise on God's part of blessing if Adam sustained his probation in obedience to God, and the promise of curse in the event of disobedience. The promise of blessing and benediction on the one hand, and that of curse and malediction on the other, are inherent in all of God's covenantal dealings. It is precisely for that reason that the entrance of sin into the world, as it occurred as a result of Adam's Fall, is to be characterized in its most straightforward terms as the repudiation of covenantal obligations.

The structure and import of God's covenantal relations with man come to focus in his covenant with Abraham and with the people through whom he chose to order his redemptive designs, the Israelites of old. The redemptive covenant unfolds its designs in the coming into the world of the Second Person of the Godhead as the Lord of the covenant to accomplish our redemption. That he did by discharging for us the obligations that rested upon us under the initial covenant of works but which, by virtue of the state of sin into which we had fallen, we were unable to discharge for ourselves. That redemptive fact lies at the heart of all that is to be said under the several doctrinal heads we shall consider. Every fact of created reality, including every fact related to our eternal redemption, is to be Christologically interpreted and understood. In short, all of the facts of reality external to the

Godhead are what they are because Christ thought them before the foundation of the world.

We begin immediately in the following chapter to consider the doctrine of God in his being and attributes and the possibility and benefits of the knowledge of God.

Chapter 2

God, His Being and Attributes

The possibility of the knowledge of God and his redemptive purpose provides the first reason for the study of Christian doctrine. Here, as at all points, we are interested in the content of the biblical revelation that conveys the substance of Christian doctrine to us. But the study of doctrine has not realized its true objective until it has exhibited the bearing of doctrine on the Christian life. Our interest lies in the pursuit and achievement of holiness, consistent with the status to which the Christian has been raised by the redemption that Christ accomplished. To that end, nothing is more practical than biblical doctrine, soundly understood and held in biblical proportion. Its imperatives for the Christian life, in its conduct and prospects, come consistently into focus.

As to the knowledge of God, the apostle John has reminded us of its imperative in his record of our Lord's High Priestly prayer: "This is life eternal, that they might know thee, the only true God" (John 17:3). If the demands and the promise of that objective are to be met, three questions arise. First, does God exist? Second, if God exists, what is it possible to know regarding his nature and character? And third, what relations exist between God and the world?

The knowledge of the being of God

We have taken the statement that *God is* as our basic apologetic and theological presupposition. At the very beginning of the Scriptural revelation God announces that he is. The Scriptures nowhere supply or suggest a proof that God exists. It was noted in the previous chapter that various attempts have been made to establish certain so-called proofs of the existence of God. But those "proofs" have themselves been disproved on logical grounds and need not detain us further. If it were possible to plug the logical holes those "proofs" contain, the best that could be said is that they establish the existence of a god made in man's image. We should not thereby have established access to God who has revealed himself in the Scriptures and in his Son whom he has sent into the world. Our interest, rather, is in what is to be said of the fact, clearly stated in God's revelation and confirmed by human experience, that every person knows that God is. We look briefly at the relevant scriptural data.

Every individual knows with an instinctive awareness that God exists. In that sense there are no atheists. Practical atheists there may be, people who live as though there is no God, who flee from the conviction of God and live the lie that God does not exist. But from the sense of God that rises uncalled in the human soul there is no escape. The apostle elaborated the point indelibly in the first chapter of his letter to the Romans. "The wrath of God is revealed from heaven against [those] who hold the truth in unrighteousness [or who willfully suppress the truth]." But how can that be said to be so? The revelation continues: "Because that which may be known of God is manifest in them; for God hath shewed it unto them." As a result of that divine demonstration, "the invisible things of him are clearly seen, being understood by the things that are made, even his eternal power and Godhead, so that they are without excuse" (Rom. 1:18-20). The statement is extensive in its insistence and in its implications for the explanation of human experience. All people know, with an awareness born in their very consciousness, and with an innateness established in their created identity, that God is; and further, that awareness places on the persons God made in his image the obligation of covenantal obedience. God has embedded in the human soul the consciousness of that obligation and the conviction of delinquency it carries with it. As the twentieth verse of that first chapter of the letter to the Romans has stated, all people not only know that God is, but they know his "eternal power and Godhead."

But what is the natural reaction to that awareness and revelation? The reaction is what it is by reason of the state of sin in which we all naturally exist, apart from the renewing, redeeming grace of God. That state devolves upon all individuals as a result of Adam's Fall. The indictment is damning in its comprehensiveness. The apostle said to the philosophers at Athens that "in him [God] we live, and move, and have our being" (Acts 17:28). God is man's environment. And from the God-consciousness innate in the human soul there is no escape. But the reality is that whenever the awareness of God rises to the surface of unregenerate consciousness it is suppressed, beaten down again, and pushed below the level of disrupting conviction. The statement we have just inspected from the letter to the Romans is explicit in its indictment. Those who live in "ungodliness and unrighteousness ... hold the truth in unrighteousness" (Rom. 1:18); or, that is, they suppress the truth and the conviction it carries with it. For that reason, the text goes on to say that God has given them up to all kinds of uncleanness. Man in his natural state is a God-hater (Rom. 1:30). What a sorry state we have been reduced to! What magnificence, what grace and mercy, is then set forth in the purpose of God to rescue his people from that cursed entailment and to bring them to the state of redemption in and by Christ his Son.

The question may be asked: If God exists, how has he revealed himself? Our discussion to this point has focused, first, on God's revelation in the word he has given in the Scriptures; and second, on his revelation of himself in the constitution of man whom he made in his image. It can be said in broader terms that God has revealed himself and his purposes also in the reality external to the Godhead that he spoke into existence, in his overruling providence and government of the course of human history, and finally in his Son.

The very heavens "declare the glory of God; and the firmament sheweth his handiwork" (Ps. 19:1). And we have seen the apostle Paul make the same claim in his letter to the Romans. Man, by reason of his creation as the image of God is himself revelatory of God. Adam's derivative personhood, which establishes his creation as the image of God, declares that God is a personal God. Adam's conscious possession of the faculties of thought, emotion, and will speaks eloquently that those capacities derive from a thinking, feeling, loving, purposeful, and gracious God. And the fact that our first parents immediately knew and lived in communion with God declares that God is a covenant-making God. Moreover, Adam's subjection to the probationary rule that he should not eat of the forbidden tree, under the promises of blessing in the event of obedience and of curse in the event of disobedience, declares that God is a God of justice. The outcome declares God to be faithful to his promise. But Adam's derivative personhood declares also that God is a God of grace. The probation under which Adam was placed carried with it the promise that by his obedience to the obligations of the creation covenant he would have been confirmed in righteousness and warranted the blessing of benediction, and not the malediction and curse that his repudiation of the covenant entailed. That promise was confirmed by the availability to our first parents of the tree of life. That was a sacrament confirmatory of God's faithfulness. An early and important theologian who flourished as a successor of Calvin in Geneva following the Reformation, Francis Turretin, observed that the tree "was a sacrament and symbol of the immortality which would have been bestowed on Adam if had persevered in his first state.... As often as he tasted its fruit, he was bound to recollect that he had life not from himself, but from God."[1]

We know that "No man hath seen God at any time; the only begotten Son, which is in the bosom of the Father, he hath declared him" (John 1:18). The Son of God came into the world as Jesus Christ, from the eternal bosom of the Father, to declare, or to reveal, the Father to us. He could say to his disciple Philip as the end of his earthly ministry neared, "He that hath seen me hath seen the Father" (John 14:9). "God, who at sundry times and in diverse manners spake in times past unto the fathers by the prophets," the writer to the Hebrews states, "hath in these days spoken unto us by his Son" (1:1-2). Christ came, full of grace and truth. He has revealed the character, the purpose, and the grace and mercy of God to us.

When we say that in these several ways God has made a self-disclosure and a revelation of his will and purpose, we note two aspects of that revelation. First, man was established at creation as the image of God and endowed with a derivative personhood analogous to the personhood of God. He naturally knew God. For Adam, to be was to know. But because he was created as a finite creature, a revelation from God was necessary in that by it God revealed himself to man and called him into communion with himself. Second, not only was revelation thereby necessary, but it was, and continues to be, clear. It is, in itself, sufficient to impress on the consciousness of man the fact that God exists, that he is the Creator, and that man therefore sustains an obligation to him. For those reasons, the revelation that God has made is authoritative. It necessarily makes the demand on man that he should recognize his total dependence on God and his consequent obligation to what God has communicated to him and requires of

---

[1] Francis Turretin, *Institutes of Elenctic Theology* (Phillipsburg, PA.: P&R Publishing, 1992), vol. 1, 581.

him. The revelation that God has given in its various forms and aspects is, we can say, necessary, authoritative, sufficient, and clear.

It follows that if people as they now survey God's creation do not recognize and glorify him as God, the fault does not in any sense lie in a defect in the revelation. The fault, rather, is in man himself as he now exists. God has implanted in the human soul both a sense of God (a *sensus deitatis*) and a seed of religion (a *semen religionis*). But that sense of God is suppressed unless the regenerating grace of God intervenes. The revelation will be clearly and properly understood only as we have the benefit of the light of the Scriptures upon it, and only as we see that as a result of the regenerating work of the Spirit of God within us.

We draw a distinction between the necessity of revelation as such and the necessity of Scripture. The necessity of revelation, we have seen, stems from the very nature of our created status. Our first parents as created were endowed with an intrinsic holiness and righteousness, though they were, as has been seen, mutable. It was possible for them not to fall into sin, but it was possible for them to fall and in doing so to repudiate the obligations of the covenant in which God had established them. The outcome of their probation is all too clear. They were finite, but their finitude is not to be confused with sin. The cause of their sin is not to be traced to any imperfection or disability inherent in their finitude. But when they had fallen, it was necessary that God should give to them, and to us who have descended from them, a written record of his revelation. Not entrusting that revelation to oral transmission, with the potential defects and deficiencies which that would entail, God has given us his written word. In it he has explained clearly his purposes of redemption from the entailment of sin to which we were subject. We can say by way of summary that the necessity of a *revelation* from God is due to our finitude, but the necessity of *Scripture* is due to our sin. And in the Scriptures we have clearly before us all that is necessary to our eternal bliss and joy in union with Christ our redeemer, to whom, by his grace, God has called us.

The knowledge of the attributes of God

Our answer to the first question, then, is that in the very act of self-awareness every person is aware of God. But our interest is not simply in the question or possibility *that* God is. We wish to know *who* God is and what he has revealed regarding his nature and character, what self-disclosure he has made. That, we shall see, takes us to the very core of belief that defines the Christian confession and life. We are asking a question similar to that of the Westminster Shorter Catechism, "What is God?" The answer follows that "God is a Spirit, infinite, eternal, and unchangeable, in his being, wisdom, power, holiness, justice, goodness, and truth."[2] In that statement the Westminster catechists have directed our thought to the attributes of God whereby he has made himself known.

In the history of the church the question has arisen as to whether a distinction can properly be drawn between the *essence* and the *attributes* of God. The response has been that as to his essence, God is incomprehensible. We know God, not because we can comprehend him in either his being or his knowledge. Rather, we know God by virtue of his self-disclosure in the attributes of being and character that he has revealed. It is true that we have available to us only a partial revelation of God's being and knowledge. In the very nature of the case it is not possible that in the finiteness of mind that defines us we could grasp and absorb and encompass a complete understanding of God who exists in his eternally glorious essence. By God's objective revelation, nevertheless, we have available to us the partial disclosure of himself that he has made. That revelation is capsuled prominently in the Scriptures he has given and preserved for our guidance. But

[2] Westminster Shorter Catechism, Question 4.

the Scriptures themselves contain only a partial record of what God has revealed in the course of human history. And further, in our finiteness and state of sin we are able to grasp only a partial understanding of that partial record. But it is to be said also that the knowledge of God that is available to us is a true knowledge, even though necessarily it is not comprehensive and total knowledge. In more technical terms, the knowledge we have of God is analogical of the knowledge that God has of himself. That means that our knowledge is like God's knowledge, but is not identical to God's knowledge.

We pause to reflect on two aspects of the knowledge that is thus available and attainable. First, while we do not have immediate access to the *essence* of God, his essence is displayed to us in his attributes of which the catechism we referred to has spoken. Turretin has observed, "The divine attributes are the essential properties by which [God] makes himself known ... they ... are attributed to him ... in order to explain his nature. Attributes are not ascribed to God properly as something superadded to his essence." By the recognition of the attributes of God as he has revealed himself to us in them we have, as Turretin goes on to state, "inadequate [incomplete and imperfect] conceptions of the essence of God."[3] The essence of God, that is who and what he is in himself, is then displayed in his attributes. When the catechism states that God is infinite, eternal, and unchangeable, it means that God is infinite, eternal, and unchangeable in each of the attributes it then goes on to mention.

Second, we have in the summary statement of the catechism a distinction between what are referred to as the *communicable* and the *incommunicable* attributes of God. By the latter are meant those attributes of God, or aspects of his being and essence, that cannot be communicated to us his creatures in the sense that we could be said to share them with him. The catechism refers to God as "infinite, eternal, and

---

[3] Turretin, op. cit., 187-88.

unchangeable," or, that is, to God's infinity, eternity, and immutability. The nature of the God-man relation is such that the creature cannot partake of infinity, eternity, and immutability. We are created as the image of God. But we are finite, temporal, and mutable. The catechism, however, speaks of divine attributes that *are* communicable to us. It speaks of God's wisdom, power, holiness, justice, goodness, and truth. In respects that we should note carefully, those attributes are communicable, and by the ministry of God's Holy Spirit they are communicated, to those whom God has redeemed.

But what, then, is involved in such a communication of attributes? Simply put, it has reference initially to that sovereign act of regeneration by which the Spirit of God creates new life within the sinner and turns him to see salvation in Christ. In that act a process of divine communication is established by which that person is progressively changed to partake of and to exhibit certain characteristics of God himself. The very conception is startling in its implications and import. To contemplate the reality involved is, of course, impossible to those who remain unmoved by the Spirit of God. Of them it is said that "the natural man receiveth not the things of the Spirit of God; for they are foolishness unto him; neither can he know them, because they are spiritually discerned" (1 Cor. 2:14). When the sinner is "born again," to use the descriptive language and the words that Christ spoke to Nicodemus (John 3:3), the new life implanted within the individual flowers into a progressive exhibition of the attributes of which we are now speaking. The individual to whom the renewing, regenerating grace of God has come will progressively exhibit something of the divine characteristics of wisdom, holiness, justice, goodness, and truth. The processes of that development will be noted more fully when we speak of the work of the Holy Spirit in the sanctification of those whom he brings to repentance and faith in Christ.

That process of the individual's progressive development should not be allowed to mean or imply the divinization of the person. Regeneration and its introduction of the sinner into union with Christ does not mean that we become divine. We do not become little gods. It is true that the apostle Peter has said that the Christian person has been made by God's "divine power" a "partaker of the divine nature" (2 Peter 1:3-4). But what is at issue there is, as we are now observing, the communication to the Christian of the graces and attributes of God. Turretin again put the matter by saying that the communicable attributes of God are "predicated analogically" of the individual.[4] By that it is meant that the Christian person is being made like God in those certain respects. He is being changed to reflect more of the character of God. He will progressively exhibit more of those divine characteristics in a likeness to God as disclosed in Christ our redeemer.

In the communication of attributes we are now referring to, God himself is sovereign in his action, as he is in the ordination of the results. While we leave aside for the present much of what is involved in God's action in that process of the Christian person's progressive sanctification, one further point can be made. God, in his sovereign conferral of his benefits and blessing on his people, is at work by his Spirit communicating his attributes and character to them to the extent that, and in the degree that, he is preparing each of them for the place he has ordained they should occupy in the eternal reign of glory with him. That is why we observed in the previous chapter that the Christian is an eschatological person. He has been assured that an inheritance of glory with Christ his redeemer has been prepared for him. Joined to Christ in the organic, vital, spiritual, and indissoluble union of which we have spoken, his eternal destiny is secure. He will come at last to "the measure of the stature of the fullness of Christ" (Eph. 4:13).

For that reason we underlined at the beginning the fact that the true objective of Christian doctrine is not realized

---

[4] Ibid., 190.

until its implications for Christian life are recognized. It follows from what has been said that the very realization that God is at work in the Christian's life, communicating to him or her something of the very attributes of God in the process of sanctification, places upon us each the responsibility to pursue with all diligence a progressive conformation to the likeness of Christ. The apostle to the Gentiles made the point by saying, "Work out your own salvation with fear and trembling. For it is God which worketh in you both to will and to do of his good pleasure" (Phil. 2:12-13). In that apostolic command we have the fact and inevitability of the Christian's progress in holiness and the urgent necessity and responsibility upon him to pursue his sanctification. That process is motivated by the realization that the Holy Spirit of God is at work in his life to accomplish that very objective. That is why the same apostle could say to the Corinthian church, and thereby to us his people, that God is at work in their lives making Christ to be to them "wisdom and righteousness and sanctification and redemption" (1 Cor. 1:30).

The triune God

That God exists as a trinity of Persons is spread clearly across the pages of Scripture. When the Westminster catechists asked the question, "How many Persons are there in the Godhead," they answered, "There are three persons in the Godhead; the Father, the Son, and the Holy Ghost; and these three are one God, the same in substance, equal in power and glory."[5] The fact and doctrine of the trinitarian consubstantiality of the Godhead that is there set before us do not need elaboration for the Christian believer. And it is not necessary to inspect in detail the copious Scripture that establishes the doctrine. The doctrine of the existence of God as three persons and as one God lies at the foundation of Christian

---

[5] Westminster Shorter Catechism, Question 6.

belief. The Scriptures do not set out to "prove" that doctrine. In fact, they do not state it in any one place in a systematic way. They leave us to conclude, by piecing together all that they say about the Personhood of God, that God exists as three Persons and as one God.

The relevant Scriptural texts are of two kinds. First, certain texts speak explicitly of the separate identity and works of the Father, the Son, and the Holy Spirit. Christ stated on one occasion, "All things are delivered to me of my Father; and no man knoweth who the Son is, but the Father; and who the Father is, but the Son" (Luke 10:22). And on another occasion he declared, "I and my Father are one" (John 10:30). When one of his disciples said to our Lord, "shew us the Father, and it sufficieth us," Christ replied, "he that hath seen me hath seen the Father" (John 14:8-9). "All that the Father giveth me shall come to me" (John 6:37). The texts could be multiplied. Christ referred explicitly also to the Holy Spirit as the third Person of the Godhead when he said to his disciples that the "Spirit of truth" would come to them (John 16:13), at the same time as he said to them, "I go to the Father" (John 16:16). Christ referred to the Holy Spirit as "the Comforter ... whom the Father will send in my name" (John 14:26).

The second class of texts explicitly attribute Personhood to each of the members of the Godhead, as, for example, in the last-cited text above where the personal pronoun "whom" is used to designate the Holy Spirit. And the personal pronoun is used for the same purpose when it is said that "when *he* is come, *he* will reprove the world of sin" (John 16:8). Christ explained the unique work of the Spirit in his statement to the disciples: "He shall glorify me: for he shall receive of mine, and shall shew it unto you" (John 16:14). The personhood of the Father and the Son are beyond dispute in the extensive testimony of the Scriptures to the redemptive work that was designed in the eternal council of the Godhead. Suffice it to say that "God sent his only begotten Son into the world ... to be the propitiation for our sins" (1 John 4:10).

Further, the unity of, and the equality between, the three Persons of the Godhead is established by the terms of the great commission, where the instruction is given to teach and baptize "in the name of the Father, and of the Son, and of the Holy Ghost" (Matt. 28:19). We should note there that the formula refers to the "name," not the "names," of the Persons of the Godhead. The text is carefully stated and conveys important doctrine to us. If the plural form of "names" had been used, the erroneous impression could have been conveyed that three Gods, not one, were referred to. The unity and simplicity of God is thus carefully preserved. If, on the other hand, the formula had referred to "the Father, Son, and Holy Ghost," the erroneous impression might follow that here we have reference to three aspects or emanations or powers of the one God. The latter would tend to reinforce an early heresy known as Sabellianism.[6] On the contrary, the reference to "the *name* of the Father and of the Son and of the Holy Ghost" carefully preserves the distinction of the three divine Persons.

The eternity, the pre-existence, and the self-existence of the Son, as the second Person of the Godhead, was, of course, under attack in the early church, and theologians such as the worthy Athanasius strenuously defended the doctrine against the relevant heresies.[7] Our interest at present is in two principal implications for Christian belief and life of what has been said of God's existence as a trinity in unity.

First, we note what is to be said regarding the relation of the three Persons of the Godhead to the essence of God. We avoid the supposition that the essence of the Godhead is in some manner distributed among, or that it is shared by, the Persons considered separately. That would be a severe

---

[6] A fuller discussion is contained in Douglas Vickers, *Divine Redemption and the Refuge of Faith* (Grand Rapids: Reformation Heritage Books, 2005), chap. 1.
[7] See ibid.

misunderstanding and misrepresentation of what God has declared and disclosed of himself. We hold, as did our fathers in the early councils of the church, to the unity of God, in the important sense that the essence of God exists fully in each of the Persons. Each of the Persons, the Father, the Son, and the Holy Spirit, is fully God. Each, that is to say, is characterized by self-existence as God. In his self-disclosure in the earliest giving of his law God declared of himself, "Hear, O Israel: The Lord our God is one Lord" (Deut. 6:4). Turretin has observed, "Although there are more persons than one in God, yet there are not more natures. All persons partake of the one and the same infinite nature, not by division, but by communication."[8] Because all of the essence of the Godhead is in each of the Persons, we do not say, for example, that there is a divine mind in the Father and a divine mind in the Son, and that those divine minds concur and agree in what is deliberated. We say, though the very saying of it brings to prominence the mystery of the Godhead, that there is one divine mind that is wholly in the Father and wholly in the Son and wholly in the Holy Spirit. Mystery of mysteries, God has not withdrawn the veil and disclosed to us what, in his eternal day, he has done in and within himself in establishing himself as three Persons, in the eternal generation of the Son and the breathing forth of the Holy Spirit. The eternal works of God internal to the Godhead (the *opera ad intra*) are beyond our comprehension. We either accept the revelation of his identity that God has given and bow before him in worship and praise for who he is and what he has done, or we reject his word to us and allow our timebound logic to force us to a position of agnosticism.

A fuller exploration of the relevant theological doctrines would require us to address the self-existence of the Son and the Holy Spirit. It would be seen that the self-existence is established in each case by the truth that each of the Persons

---

[8] Turretin, op. cit., 182.

is fully God, and that God is characterized by self-existence. God exists as three persons, but he is one God. The God we know is not known except as he is known as both one and three. In our thought about God the threeness does not take precedence over the oneness, nor the oneness take precedence over the threeness. A Scottish theologian of the nineteenth century, George Smeaton, has made the point by quoting with approval the statement of the ancient church father Gregory Nazianzen, that "I cannot think of the *one* but I am immediately surrounded by the splendour of *three*; nor can I clearly discover the three, but I am suddenly carried back to the one."[9]

A final point follows from our doctrine of God in the terms in which we have inspected it. It is that by virtue of the unity and simplicity of the Godhead there does not exist a subordination of essence or being among the Persons of the Godhead. Each Person is fully God. But we may also speak of the trinity of the Godhead from a different aspect. We have already referred to a point we shall discuss in more detail, namely the distribution of redemptive offices among the three persons of the Godhead. When the trinity is viewed in that perspective, it is usual to speak of the economic trinity. The word "economic" in that aspect refers to the distribution of redemptive offices or responsibilities, or the agreed undertakings and commitments, among the divine Persons. As to the economic trinity, as distinct from the ontological trinity, or the trinity of the *being* of God, we say that a subordination of offices exists. The Son willingly subordinated himself to the will of the Father in carrying out his work of redemption. And the Holy Spirit subordinated himself to the Father and the Son in his coming into the world and into the lives of the people whom Christ redeemed. But what we are doing in these different ways is to look at the revelation of the being and

---

[9] George Smeaton, *The Doctrine of the Holy Spirit* (Edinburgh: Banner of Truth, 1974), 6.

actions of the triune Godhead from different perspectives. Within the trinity considered in its ontological aspect, there is no subordination. Subordination does occur within the relation between the Persons of the trinity as that is considered in its economic aspect, or in relation to the works of God external to the Godhead.

But why, we can properly ask, is this doctrine of the trinity of God of practical relevance to the Christian in the everyday working out of his belief and life? The question brings us to the second of the reasons we had in view for pausing to note what is involved in the doctrine. At this stage the point of relevance can be stated briefly, as we shall return to the relevant issues in more detail. We are interested in the identity of the Persons of the Godhead, in the unity and the trinity in which we have just contemplated them, because we are interested in the works of each of the Persons in the respective offices they have undertaken and performed for our redemption. That itself projects to the Christian two levels of significance.

First, the Christian believer enjoys the position in which he now stands in his union with Christ because of the work of the Father in the design of redemption before the foundation of the world. "God so loved the world, that he gave his only begotten Son, that whosoever believeth in him should not perish, but have everlasting life" (John 3:16). And the design of redemption was carried out in fact by the coming of the Son, by his perfect obedience in the life he lived in this world, and by his substitutionary sacrifice for the sins of his people. The Son came, he said, "to give his life a ransom for many" (Mark 10:45). Though "by one man's disobedience many were made sinners, so by the obedience of one shall many be made righteous" (Rom. 5:19). The work of the Holy Spirit has fulfilled, and continues to fulfill, the promise of our Lord that he, the Spirit, would apply to those whom Christ redeemed the benefits and blessings of the redemption he accomplished for them. When it is asked, "How are we made partakers of the redemption purchased by Christ?" the answer follows that it is "by the effectual application of it to us by his Holy Spirit."[10] The Spirit does that "by working faith in us, and thereby uniting us to Christ in our effectual calling."[11] We are renewed in Christ, the apostle Paul explained, "by the washing of regeneration and renewing of the Holy Ghost" (Titus 3:5).

A second and highly important point of relevance of the doctrine follows. Beyond the recognition of the works of the three Persons of the Godhead, the Christian believer sees that the very fact and reality of those works place upon him the obligation and the necessity of a response on his part. In a different but related context the apostle Peter drew the corresponding deduction, "Seeing ...these ... things ... what manner of persons ought ye to be in all holy conversation [or manner of life] and godliness" (2 Peter 3:11). The awareness of who God is, and of what God has done in his eternal wisdom and mercy to save sinners, elicits the worship and praise and love of those whom he has brought to himself in Christ. Here, in other words, we have again the motivation to the pursuit of holiness and the life of righteousness to which we are called by the God of all grace who has saved us at so great a price.

The holiness of God

In our discussion of the attributes of God we have spoken of his holiness. When we contemplate the majesty and glory and sovereignty of God, his holiness shines out as the attribute which, in a unique sense, characterizes his essential being. It is not so much as one among a sequence of attributes that we contemplate the holiness of God. Holy, we may go on to see, is what God reveals himself to be in his very essence.

---

[10] Westminster Shorter Catechism, Question 29.
[11] Ibid., Question 30.

We mean by that statement that we understand all of God's attributes to be characterized by holiness. His wisdom is a holy wisdom, his power, justice, and goodness are holy, and his wrath against sin and the sinner is a holy wrath. God's holiness is an all-comprehending description of the transcendence of God himself. It speaks of his separateness from all that exists external to him and all that has been called into existence by the word of his power. The essential meaning of holiness is that of God's separateness. He exists before all of created reality external to himself, he is the source and origin and Creator of all reality, and he alone, as Paul stated to Timothy, "hath immortality" (1 Tim. 6:16).

Stephen Charnock, a Puritan in seventeenth-century England, wrote a magnificent treatise on the existence and attributes of God. "Holiness," he says, "is a glorious perfection belonging to the nature of God; hence he is in Scripture styled the Holy One, the Holy One of Jacob, the Holy One of Israel, and oftener entitled Holy than Almighty, and set forth by this part of his dignity more than any other. This is more affixed as an epithet to his name than any other; you never find it expressed, his *mighty name* or his *wise name*, but his *great name* and most of all his *holy name*. This is his greatest title of honour; in this doth the majesty and venerableness of his name appear."[12] Charnock continues: "The nature of God cannot rationally be conceived" without holiness. Of all the characteristics or aspects of the Godhead, or of all of the respects in which God has revealed himself, "none is sounded out so loftily, with such solemnity, and so frequently by angels that stand before his throne, as this. Where do we find any other attribute trebled in the praises of it, as this? 'Holy, Holy, Holy, is the Lord of hosts; the whole earth is full of his glory' (Is. 6:3); and 'the four beasts rest not day and night saying Holy, holy, holy Lord God Almighty'" (Rev. 4:8).

---

[12] Stephen Charnock, *The Existence and Attributes of God* (Minneapolis: Klock & Klock, 1969), 448.

Charnock concludes, "Do you hear in any angelic song any other perfection of divine nature thrice repeated? Where do you read of the crying out Eternal, eternal, eternal; or Faithful, faithful, faithful, Lord God of hosts!"[13]

It is by his holiness, moreover, that God has sworn his fidelity to his promises. "Once have I sworn by my holiness," he has said in Psalm 89:35. And again, the prophet Amos declares that "The Lord God hath sworn by his holiness" (Amos 4:2). It is by the very essential Godness of his being that God swears. But the Scriptures we have just quoted from the Psalmist and from Amos make it clear that it is his holiness that is advanced as the essential descriptive character of his being.

It becomes clear that holiness is descriptive of the essence of God as he exists in himself. All of God's being and attributes are characterized by holiness. The love of God is a holy love. His wrath is a holy wrath. His truthfulness is a holy truthfulness. His justice is a holy justice. Holiness is the comprehensive and summary characteristic of God as he has revealed himself.

Holiness and righteousness

The contemplation of the holiness of God projects our thought to his righteousness. Holiness and righteousness are quite separate terms, the meanings of which have frequently been confused. The terms have been used interchangeably or as meaning essentially the same thing. That is frequently done in our thought of the holiness and righteousness of the individual. We should avoid that confusion in our statement of doctrine. We say quite properly that our first parents were created "in knowledge, righteousness, and holiness,"[14] reflecting the statement of the apostle to the Ephesians that

---

[13] Ibid., 449.
[14] Westminster Shorter Catechism, Question 10.

they should "put on the new man, which after God is created in righteousness and true holiness" (Eph. 4:24). But holiness and righteousness are to be understood as referable to different aspects of character.

It will clarify our thinking at this point if we refer to what we mean by righteousness in man as God's creature, meaning notably, of course, God's redeemed people. To summarize, holiness refers to the essential nature of being or state and condition of the regenerate person. Righteousness, on the other hand, refers not primarily to a state or condition, but to action that accords with a prior condition. It is a characteristic of action, which in turn is said to be righteous in so far as it is consistent with the inherently holy nature and quality or character of the one performing the act. One is holy by virtue of the state in which he exists. He is righteous because his actions are of a certain kind or character as seen in relation to that state.

In the case of the individual person this important distinction is crystallized by saying that one is righteous if, and in so far as, his or her relation to the law of God is what it ought to be. Holding, then, to the notion that righteousness in its essential reference to action consists in conformity to law, the question arises whether we can similarly understand the righteousness of God as being related to law. The answer is that we should do precisely that.

In speaking of the holiness of God we have had reference to his transcendence or his separateness. When we contemplate the very nature of being and reality we hold in view a twofold approach to explanation. First, there is God. And second, there is reality external to the Godhead that God spoke into existence. God is separate, distinct, from all that he has made, and in his eternal self-existence he is not dependent in any respect on any thing or law external to himself, either for the explanation of his own being or his knowledge. That separateness is the first connotation of his holiness. That concept of separateness is of the essence of the meaning of holiness in all of its expressions. We should bear in mind also, then, the aspect of God's holiness that we may refer to as his consistency, meaning by that the fact that all of God's thoughts, designs, actions, expressions, and revelations are consistent, as to their character and intention, with the nature and being of God as he has declared himself to exist. This aspect of God's character that we refer to as his consistency can be designated his righteousness.

It follows from all we have said regarding the character and the holiness of God that it is impossible that God could be, or could have been, subject to, or answerable to, a law external to or higher than himself. If we were to imagine that God, as well as man, was subject to separately defined laws or standards of goodness, then we should have to say that God was no longer God. If all that we have said in our doctrine of God to this point is true, then there could not have been a law or any other category or standard of meaning external to, or higher than, God, which could have determined the quality or character of God's being, his knowledge, and his acting.

But if we are to be consistent in our definitions, we say that righteousness as it is ascribed to God continues to consist in conformity to law. But the law that is thereby in view is the law of God's own being and perfections. In all that he thinks, determines, wills, and performs, God is faithful to himself and the requirements of his own holiness and glory. God "cannot deny himself" (2 Tim. 2:11). All of God's determinations and actions are consistent with the immutability of his character.

The transcendence and immanence of God

In our references to the holiness of God we have had in view what is referred to as his transcendence or his separateness from the world. We take note now of what is referred to as God's immanence, or his relations with, and his actions within, the world. The important concept of immanence takes up God's participation, by his continuing government and providence, in the history of the world that he called into existence. In that, as in the creation at the beginning, God is sovereign in all that comes to pass. We concur with the statement of the catechism that "God's works of providence are his most holy, wise, and powerful preserving and governing all his creatures, and all their actions."[15] Those works of providence implement his decrees, understood as "his eternal purpose, according to the counsel of his will, whereby, for his own glory, he hath foreordained whatsoever comes to pass."[16]

God's immanence follows from his incommunicable attributes of infinity and omnipresence, which means that there is not a speck of space or an instant of time which God does not occupy. He is immanently at work by his power and by the operation of his Holy Spirit in all things and all people at all times and all occasions, working and willing to do of his good pleasure. "By him all things consist" (Col. 1:17). He is present in all the good and in all the evil, though he is not the author of sin. Consider the remark of Joseph who, after he had revealed his identity to his brothers during the Egyptian famine, said to them that notwithstanding their having sold him into slavery some years previously, "Ye thought evil against me; but God meant it unto good, to bring to pass, as it is this day, to save much people alive" (Gen. 50:20). Amos 3:6 states: "Shall there be evil in a city, and the Lord hath not done it?" And it is equally clearly stated that God moved in and dealt with the heart of Pharaoh according to his purpose in the final liberation of the Israelites from their slavery in Egypt (Rom. 9:17).

A respected nineteenth century writer, Archibald Alexander Hodge of Princeton Theological Seminary, has made the point of doctrine as eloquently as any writer. He observes that God "transcends all the limitations of space and time. He is everywhere present in his eternal essence. The whole

---

[15] Westminster Shorter Catechism, Question 11.
[16] Ibid., Question 7.

essence, with all its inherent properties is present at every moment of time to every point of space.... All creatures exist, and act only as they exist, in him.... 'In him all things live and move and have their being'; he turneth the hearts of men even as rivers of water are turned; he worketh in us to will and to do of his own good pleasure.... The fact that the whole indivisible God is eternally in each point of space transcends our understanding ... his whole infinite being dwells everlastingly in each atom and each spirit."[17]

What we say, then, is that God, by the operation of his Holy Spirit, is immanently active in all of the eventuation of all of reality external to himself. He works, not only upon, but within, all entities and persons within the reality that he has established and structured. That is mystery indeed. But the fact that the mystery of it transcends our thought and our capacities for thought in no sense warrants us to overlook or to diminish its reality and importance.

Finally, we should see again the meaning and the significance of the immanent grace of God for our progress and development in the Christian life. It is a wonderful and encouraging truth that God, by the sovereign design and working of his Holy Spirit, is immanently at work in the lives of his people, preparing them for glory, and bringing them infallibly to reign with Christ their redeemer in the eternal kingdom that he has gone to prepare for them. May his people give all diligence to follow in the ways of righteousness in the grace that he has so lavishly bestowed.

---

[17] A. A. Hodge, *Evangelical Theology* (Edinburgh: Banner of Truth, 1976), 25, 35.

Chapter 3

The Biblical Revelation and the Knowledge of God

We have spoken in the preceding chapter of the forms of God's revelation and the manner in which he has made himself known. A revelation and communication from God was necessary by reason of our finitude. But given that the first man, Adam, was established as our federal head and the representative of the race, we were involved in the guilt of his first sin. In the darkness and ignorance that descended as a result, it was necessary that God should make a revelation in written form and that what he had to say to man should be inscripturated for our permanent instruction and guidance. The Scriptures, in the canonical form in which we now possess them, stand as the Word of God and as our ultimate source of revelation. They provide our standard, criterion, and test of truth and belief. They are authoritative in relation to everything of which they speak; and they speak of all things necessary to our understanding of life in this world and in that which is to come. We want to know, then, why we believe that the Bible is the Word of God, why it is our trustworthy source of revelation, and why, as a result, it conveys to us the only infallible rule of life. Our immediate concern is with the reliability of the biblical revelation.

It is not possible in the present space to attempt a full exploration of that important question. A copious literature exists on the various aspects of the doctrine of the scripturicity of Scripture. It is important to observe that in the same way as we are bound to the Scriptural doctrine on all matter related to our faith, we are bound to the Scriptural doctrine of Scripture. In making that statement we are not arguing in a circle, as a fuller demonstration of the grounds for it will confirm. But a full apologetic defense of the claim is beyond our present objective. At the risk again of leaving far too many worthy names aside, a minimum introduction to the fuller discussion of the relevant questions exists in works by Packer,[1] Young,[2] Van Til,[3] Weeks,[4] and Warfield.[5]

The Scriptures inerrant, infallible, authoritative, and verbally inspired

Our doctrine of Scripture states that the Bible *is*, and not that it merely *contains*, the Word of God. In all that it says, the Bible is inerrant, infallible, authoritative, and verbally and fully inspired. The Bible is authoritative in relation to everything of which it speaks. And it is important for us to see that

---

[1] J. I. Packer, *'Fundamentalism' and the Word of God* (Grand Rapids: Eerdmans, 1958).
[2] Edward J. Young, *Thy Word is Truth* (Grand Rapids: Eerdmans, 1957).
[3] Cornelius Van Til, *The Protestant Doctrine of Scripture* (Phillipsburg: Presbyterian and Reformed, 1967).
[4] Noel Weeks, *The Sufficiency of Scripture* (Edinburgh: Banner of Truth, 1988).
[5] B. B. Warfield, *The Inspiration and Authority of the Bible* (Philadelphia: Presbyterian and Reformed Publishing, 1967). Relevant questions are addressed also in Douglas Vickers, *Christian Confession and the Crackling Thorn* (Grand Rapids: Reformation Heritage Books, 2004), chap. 6, "The Necessity and Canonicity of Scripture."

the Bible speaks of everything. It doesn't, of course, speak of everything directly, because, for example, it says nothing about baseball games and how to service automobiles. But we should not hesitate to say that the Bible speaks of everything indirectly, if not directly. That includes all conceivable facts and relations within the created reality that God spoke into existence by the word of his power. For the Bible tells us who God who made all things is, who we are, and what we have available to us as the true categories of understanding and interpretation. Further and in the light of that, the Bible explains what the interpretation of all things according to its categories implies for the way we live.

Such a claim, deliberately comprehensive as it is, is supported by what we stated at an earlier point. That was the claim that as we observe and set out to interpret and understand the universe of reality in which we find ourselves, we acknowledge that all of the facts we encounter are God's facts. All of the facts are what they are because God thought them before the foundation of the world. There are no brute facts. Or, that is to say, there are no uninterpreted facts. By that we mean that all of the facts are already interpreted by reason of the place they occupy in God's eternal plan for this world and universe and all that is in it. Because that is so, our task is not to make what we imagine is an original and constructive interpretation of reality. Our task is to endeavor, by the grace of God and the light of his Spirit, to become aware of the proper reinterpretation of the facts that God has already interpreted.

The meaning of verbal inspiration

The terms in which the Bible as the Word of God has been described need to be carefully understood. Take first the claim that the Bible is verbally inspired. We mean by that, not only that the Bible is in some general sense consistent with what God intended to convey to us. We mean to say that the very words of the Bible, in all their individuality and particularity in the original autographs, are the words of God. That, of course, should make us careful to guard the very words of the Bible, in the sense that it influences our attitude to the translation of the Scriptures and the procedures we adopt in translating into our own language the words that God gave in the original languages in which the autographs were written. We should accordingly be careful not to place undue weight in, or give undue credence to, those so-called translations of the Scriptures that are essentially paraphrases of the text, rather than real and actual translations.

The claim of verbal inspiration does not mean, as some opponents of the doctrine have caricatured it, that God dictated the Scriptures. The Bible is, of course, a human document, in the obvious sense that its immediate authors were human persons. But two statements of the Scriptures themselves clarify what was involved in the writing of the Bible. Paul states in his letter to Timothy, "All scripture is given by inspiration of God," or, that is, all Scriptures have been "breathed out" by God (2 Tim. 3:16). And Peter tells us: "Holy men of God spake as they were moved by the Holy Ghost" (2 Peter 1:21). The human authors of the Scriptures, it is being said, were carried along by the Holy Spirit in writing what they did.

The obvious matter of immediate human authorship must be seen in the light of the fact that God so overruled in all aspects of the preparation of those authors, as to their personal histories, education, formal or otherwise, temperament, literary style, and life-awareness, that the words they wrote under the inspiration of his Holy Spirit were precisely the words that God intended to be written. Those words, then, are the very words of God, as they appear in the original autographs that the human authors produced.

The Scriptural autographs and textual criticism

We do not, of course, possess those original autographs at this time. What we have are copies, and copies of copies. It would be a long, though a very interesting and important, digression to discuss the ways in which the discipline of textual criticism has been at work to make as certain as possible that the texts as we now have them are virtually the original texts. There are in existence, for example, about 5,000 parts of the New Testament Greek manuscripts that make up the New Testament text that we read in our present-day Bibles. The remarkable thing about those manuscripts is the very high degree of agreement among them as to the actual words they contain. Only a miniscule number of variations exist between them, and virtually all that remain are differences of orthography (spelling of words).

We take only one example from the Scriptures that might be of interest. A difference of view exists among scholars whether the word in Luke 2:14 that is translated as "good will" or "good pleasure" was written in the original autograph in the nominative case or in the genitive. The spelling of those two cases differs only slightly. But if we take the nominative, we understand the text to speak of "good will toward men" (KJV and NKJV). If, however, we take the genitive case, we read the text as speaking of "men with whom he [God] is pleased" (NASB), or "men on whom his favor rests" (NIV).

The providential preservation of Scripture

But in our Bibles as we now have them, to the extent that they have been translated from the original texts with a careful awareness that the words of the text are the words of God, we have a true, inerrant, infallible, authoritative statement of what God intended to convey to us. The Bible as we have it provides us with a reliable and trustworthy statement of the doctrines of the Christian faith. The doctrinal content of the

Scriptures is not jeopardized by the minor differences that exist between the parts of the original language texts that have been preserved. Attention can be drawn, moreover, to another important aspect of our doctrine of Scripture. The *Westminster Confession of Faith* and the *Savoy Declaration of Faith* both say that the Scriptures "at the time of writing" were "immediately inspired by God, *and by his singular care and providence kept pure in all ages*, [and they] are therefore authentic." What is being said is that the providence of God has preserved to us all that we need in order to have before us, as the Confession states it, "the whole counsel of God, concerning all things necessary for his own glory, man's salvation, faith, and life, ... expressly set down in scriptures, or by good and necessary consequences [they] may be deduced from scripture."[6]

The necessity, authority, sufficiency, and perspicuity of Scripture

The doctrine of Scripture can be summarized further in the following way. We observed earlier that God's revelation in the universe of nature was necessary, authoritative, sufficient, and perspicuous. When we say that the revelation is "perspicuous," we are saying that it is a clear revelation, meaning that it can be clearly understood. We confronted at that earlier point the question why all people do not see clearly and understand and believe the revelation. We concluded that there was no fault or defect in the revelation itself, but that the defect in the failure to understand and believe was in the person himself. That defect existed because of the state of sin to which we were reduced by Adam's Fall. But when, as a result of the regenerating and enlightening work of the Holy Spirit, we are enabled to see clearly again, the being and

---

[6] *The Westminster Confession of Faith*, various editions, chap. 1.

perfections of God shine clearly from all that exists in the universe of nature.

The revelation of God as we have it in the Scriptures is necessary, authoritative, sufficient, and perspicuous. That follows from what has been said so far regarding the doctrine of Scripture. But the following point might be made. We have referred to the *necessity* of Scripture. It can now be said that the *authority* of Scripture and, along with that, the *sufficiency* of it, follows from its necessity. We may expand our previous statement by observing that the necessity of Scripture is grounded in two reasons. First, the state of sin and darkness into which we had fallen made it necessary that God should give us a full, clear, written statement of his law as our rule of life, the continual investigation of which would make our relation to him perfectly clear to us. It would by that means clarify and codify our obligations to God as our Creator and redeemer, and it would make clear the manner in which, in fulfilling those obligations, we should live in such a way as to please him. We say, then, that the fact that God gave us a written, or, as we have said, an inscripturated revelation, was an accommodation to our fallen condition and our fallen capacities of soul.

Second, it was necessary that God should give to the world a written revelation in order that there would be a permanent record of his law and of the requirements of his covenantal relations with mankind. God's law as he gave it to his people through Moses contained a large amount of what we refer to as ceremonial and civil or judicial law. Those aspects of the law have been fulfilled in Christ. They have therefore passed away, in the sense that the institutional structures in which they earlier came to expression are no longer mandatory. But it is important to emphasize that God also gave a moral law. That was encapsulated in the Ten Commandments and it was, in its essence, a republication or a rearticulation of the law as God had given it to Adam at the beginning. Among the so-called creation ordinances that God gave to Adam were the mandates that reappear in written form in the decalogue, or the Ten Commandments. Adam was given, as the earliest chapters of Genesis make clear, mandates or laws regarding marriage, work, worship, economic responsibility, social relations, and the Sabbath. Because the Ten Commandments are a republication of the moral law that was given to Adam at the beginning, they continue to define what God requires of people in general. At the same time they are, of course, the rule of life for God's people.

The partial nature of God's revelation

It is necessary, even in the present brief survey, to note two further aspects of God's inscripturated revelation. First, God has given to us as his creatures a partial revelation of himself, of his being, essence, attributes, and purposes. We say, as we noted briefly at an earlier point, that God has given us a partial revelation because in the very nature of the Creator-creature relation and distinction that exists, it is not possible that we could have a comprehensive knowledge of God. We have a true knowledge of God and his ways, but not a comprehensive knowledge. We can say, further, that in the Scriptures we have a partial record of the partial revelation that God has made. That is beautifully borne out by the statement of the apostle John in the very last verse of his gospel when he said, "There are also many other things which Jesus did, the which, if they should be written every one, I suppose that even the world itself could not contain the books that should be written" (John 21:25). Similarly, it is not necessarily the case that the prophets and historians of old have actually written down all that they heard or experienced in their communications with and from God. What we do know is that all that was written was exactly what God wished to be written in the precise words that he wished to be employed and preserved.

But not only do we have in the Scriptures a partial record

of God's partial revelation. We have, at best, only a partial understanding of that partial revelation. We have said that as a result of the regenerating work of the Holy Spirit within us, we have a true knowledge of God and his purposes. It is true knowledge, even though it is not comprehensive knowledge. But we do well to remember that our grasp and understanding of what we have revealed to us is progressive. When John wrote his first epistle he said at a certain point that he was writing to "children," then to "young men," then to "fathers." And so it is. There are progressive stages in our understanding and grasp and experience of revealed truth. As Paul put it to the Corinthians, at our best we see "through a glass darkly." The Holy Spirit will continue to guide us and expand our sanctified understanding, and in the last great day of the Lord we shall see all things with new and wider clarity.

All revelation is anthropomorphic

The second thing to be said is that all of God's revelation is anthropomorphic. The use of that technical term impresses upon us two things. First, God is not a man such as we are. We know and believe that God entered into our time and space in the incarnation of his Son. The second Person of the Godhead became man by taking our human nature, yet without sin, into union with his divine nature. But he did not become a human person. In him the human nature was not personalized. Our Lord was and remains a divine Person. We have already taken note of the reality that God is separate from us, and that he exists transcendentally separate from all of created reality external to himself. Yet he condescends to make himself immanently concerned with, and active in, the events and histories of all that exists in this world.

Second, when we say that all revelation is anthropomorphic revelation, we are saying that God speaks to us in the language of men, frequently in the form of a man, and discloses himself in analogies and relations that, as a result, engage our comprehension and understanding. God, that is, continues graciously to accommodate himself to us and to the range of capacity of comprehension we possess as created in his image. He does that in order that we shall understand what he reveals to us in the manner in which we are capable of doing so by virtue of the abilities of soul with which he endowed us.

Our understanding of the infallible revelation is not infallible

Our final comment at this preliminary point follows from what has just been said. We have before us an infallible revelation. But we can never say that we have an infallible understanding of that infallible revelation. Again we know and understand truly, but not comprehensively, or exhaustively, or completely, or infallibly. That should breed in us who belong to Christ a humility as we hold in our hands the revelation he has given. We know, as Hosea assured us, that "then shall we know, if we follow on to know the Lord" (Hos. 6:3). And we hold to the precious promise of Jeremiah, through whom God said, "I will give them an heart to know me" (Jer. 24:7). We trust in the promise of our Lord that he will continue to send his Spirit to us to "guide us into all truth" (John 16:13). We know now in part, with all the stumbling imperfections of understanding that our humanity and the residue of sin within us make us capable of, but we progress in knowledge and sanctification as God in Christ ministers his grace to us.

How do we know that the Bible is the Word of God?

What we have said has stated the essence of our doctrine of Scripture. We have seen that the Scripture makes its own claim of scripturicity. That occurs in the texts we quoted from Paul's second epistle to Timothy and the second epistle of

Peter. If we were to survey the doctrine of Scripture more exhaustively we would see that the Scriptures' own testimony to their scripturicity is, in fact, a highly significant and important part of the claims we make. But in the present space, we note a number of headings under which the doctrine of Scripture can be worked out more fully. We may observe, for example, the following:

First, the unity of the themes of Scripture, notwithstanding the fact that the 66 books that make up our Bible were written by men who were widely separated in time and distance and who lived under a variety of cultural, social, and economic conditions.

Second, the consistency between the progressive statements of the books of the Scripture as to God's revelation of his own being and nature, the state of humanity at large and of God's church in particular, and the possibility, method, and accomplishment of redemption.

Third, the sublimity of the language, as well as the majesty of the subject-content, in which, and of which, the Scriptures speak. We note the consistent authority that the Scriptures present us with: "Thus saith the Lord."

Fourth, the honesty with which the Scriptures explain the fallibilities and the sinfulness of those to whom they are addressed.

Fifth, the detail of the prophecies contained in the Scriptures and the confirmation provided by the equally detailed fulfillment of them. In Micah 5:2 we have even a precise and detailed prophesy of the place of the birth of our Lord.

Sixth, the manner in which our Lord made use of the Old Testament Scriptures, too extensive to be surveyed in detail at this point, but evidenced in such statements of his that "the Scriptures ... testify of me" (John 5:39), in his claim that he himself fulfilled the prophecy of Isaiah 61:1ff. when he spoke in the synagogue at Nazareth (Luke 4:16-21), and in his reference to Moses when he identified himself as the bread of life (John 6). Many more instances could be given. The

Scripture as it existed at the time of Christ was, of course, what we now have as our Old Testament.

Seventh, the apostles' use of, and dependence on, the Scriptures, as in, for example, Peter's sermon at Pentecost when he invoked the Old Testament claims regarding God's sovereign ordination of history and the prophecy of Joel; Stephen's rehearsal of Old Testament history at the time of his martyrdom; Paul's declaration of God's sovereignty and predestinating will in his letter to the Ephesians; Paul's reference to Mosaic history in 1 Corinthians 10; and Peter's reference to Noah in his first epistle (1 Peter 3:18f.).

Eighth, the unity and consistency of doctrine and witness of the New Testament authors. We note that Peter was actually very forthright in claiming that the writings of the apostle Paul were to be accepted as Scripture. In 2 Peter 3:16 the epistles of Paul are placed on the same level, as to their scripturicity, as "other scriptures" (KJV) or "the rest of the Scriptures" (NKJV).

The internal testimony of the Spirit

Much has been made in the history of theology of an additional ground for the claim that the Bible is the Word of God. We have the final and confirmatory proof in what is referred to as the internal testimony of the Spirit. The nature of what is involved at this point is conveyed by the statement of the Westminster Confession that "our full persuasion and assurance of the infallible truth and divine authority thereof [i.e. of the Scriptures], is from the inward work of the Holy Spirit, bearing witness by and with the word in our hearts."[7]

The doctrine of the internal testimony of the Spirit in this connection is important and needs to be carefully understood. The testimony of the Holy Spirit to the saints of God is to be observed and equally carefully understood, of course, in other

---

[7] Idem.

parts of the Scripture and in other contexts of Christian doctrine. But involved at this point is the relation between the Scriptures' self-authentication and the testimony of the Spirit.

The statement of the Confession is very judicious and carefully put. It says that the Spirit "bears witness by and with the word." The meaning of that can be put both negatively and positively. We take the negative first. It is not being said that the Holy Spirit bears what we might refer to as a "bare testimony," in the sense that he simply tells us that the Bible is the Word of God and that we should therefore regard it as such and give full credence to it. The confessional statement is very different from that. It says, first, that the Scripture bears witness to itself. That means that the Scriptures are "self-authenticating." When we make a full survey of the scripturicity of Scripture we have to become aware of, and hold to, the Scriptures' self-authentication.

But if, then, the Scriptures are self-authenticating, what remains for the work of the Holy Spirit? The answer at that point is to be seen as the crux of our doctrine. It is the positive statement that the work of the Spirit is to take away the blindness of our eyes, and to enlighten our vision, in such a way that we can now see clearly what was there to be seen all along, namely, that the Scriptures authenticate their own scripturicity. The Spirit doesn't make a bare statement to us that the Bible is the Word of God. Rather, he enables us to *see*, from all that the Scriptures say, that they *are*, in fact, the Word of God.

That, of course, is the manner of the Spirit's dealing with us in all parts and aspects of our Christian lives. In his act of regeneration the Holy Spirit does the very same thing. He operates within and upon the faculties of the soul and endows them with new abilities and capacities in such a way that the regenerate person is then able to see clearly what was always there to be seen, but which was previously foolishness to him because his eyes were blinded. The situation from which we are rescued is as Paul described it to the Corinthians: "The god of this world hath blinded the mind" (2 Cor. 4:4). But "God who commanded the light to shine out of darkness [at the original creation] hath shined in our hearts to give the light of the knowledge of the glory of God in the face of Jesus Christ" (2 Cor. 4:6). That is always the manner of God's working through the agency of his Holy Spirit. And so it is in the case we are now considering. The "internal testimony of the Spirit" takes away our blindness and enables us to see the Scriptures as the Word of God clearly before us.

The key to the Scriptures

It was observed at the conclusion of the first chapter that biblical theology is covenant theology. God's relations with man have always been covenantal relations. We shall consider at more length in the following chapter the nature of the various covenants that God has made, culminating in the covenant of grace that was directed to our redemption. The realization of the terms and dimensions of God's covenant purposes will influence all of our understanding of Christian doctrine and its application to the Christian life. The recognition of God's covenant and purpose provides the key to the understanding of the biblical revelation. In more technical terms, the recognition of God's covenantal purpose provides the fundamental hermeneutical principle in terms of which the Scriptures are to be read and understood. It is the interpretative key in terms of which we hear the Scriptures speak.

The Bible as we have it, the Word of God, is to be seen, from beginning to end, as a redemptive revelation. We shall see the meaning of that from other perspectives when we have addressed the fact and the meaning of our descent into the state of sin that followed from Adam's Fall. But when we say that we have in the Scriptures a redemptive revelation, we can say, as a result, that Christ, who came to be our redeemer, is the key to the Scriptures. He told the Jews that the Old Testament Scriptures spoke of him (John 5:39). The Christ-event, in its prophetic anticipation and then in its full realization, provides us with the key to unlocking the entire meaning of the Scriptures.

But from that follows the point with which we are at present concerned. There is no way, we must say, in which the Christ-event, or anything related to it, can be understood unless it is understood in terms of, and within the context of, the Covenant of Redemption, of which the coming of Christ was the fulfillment. Christ came as the Lord of the covenant. What we must do, therefore, if we are going to grasp the message of the Scriptures, is to grasp the meaning of the covenantal context in which all of God's relations with us are to be interpreted and understood. In short, then, as has been said, the key to the Scriptures is a covenantal key. We shall understand the Scriptures only as we understand them to be an expanded revelation of all that God has decreed and purposed and accomplished in working out and implementing the terms of his covenant with the world he made in general and with his redeemed people in particular.

The knowledge of God

It is apposite to the discussion of the biblical revelation to reflect on the knowledge of God, or the knowledge that God possesses, that lies behind his self-disclosure and the revelation he has made. When we refer to God's knowledge we have in view, first, God's knowledge of himself and his purposes, and secondly, his knowledge of all that exists and all that eventuates external to the Godhead.

It would be possible to cast our studies on a wider scale. We could speak of the *aseity* and the *immortality* of God. God exists, as we shall go on to observe, outside of time. But by virtue of his transcendent eternity we acknowledge also his aseity, meaning that his existence is independent of all that is external to himself, that it is underived or uncaused.

When we refer to God's immortality we have in view

Paul's letter to Timothy in which he includes that doxological ascription of honor and glory to "the only wise God," "the King eternal immortal, invisible" (1 Tim. 1:17). In the same letter Paul focuses our thought on "the King of kings and Lord of lords; who only hath immortality" (1 Tim. 6:15-16). When Paul speaks of the immortality of God he is taking up again aspects of what we have referred to as God's aseity. He is saying in another way that God's existence is not derived from any more ultimate cause than himself.

When we say, then, that God alone has immortality, we are directing our thought to two things. First, the immortality of God has reference not primarily to time and its possible ending or non-ending, but to a condition of God's existence outside of time. Second, God himself is the creator of the immortality which, as analogical of his own existence, he has bestowed on those of his creatures whom he has made in his image. For them the temporal process in which they exist will, in fact, be non-ending. The prefix "im" in immortality, as it is here referred to God, is designed to convey our thought away completely from the region in which mortality or death in time can be contemplated. Our contemplation of God, on the contrary, cannot legitimately raise the category of mortality in the sense that, in relation to him, the ending or non-ending of time could be contemplated as possible or not possible. The prefix has removed us completely from any such level of consideration. The awareness of God, as the apostle here directs us to it, has reference to a plane of God's existence that has nothing at all to do with the dimensions or possible structures, or the beginning or ending, of time.

We could speak also of the *immensity* of God. In doing so, we would align our thought with that of Solomon, who acknowledged in his cry to God that "the heaven and heaven of heavens cannot contain thee" (1 Kings 8:27). The same recognition of the transcendent being of God is reflected in the words of the chronicler (2 Chron. 2:6). The prophet Isaiah takes up the theme of God's immensity and observes in the final chapter of his prophecy, "Thus saith the Lord, the heaven is my throne, and the earth is my footstool" (Is. 66:1). Again, God says through the prophet Jeremiah, "Can any hide himself in secret places that I shall not see him? ... Do not I fill heaven and earth? saith the Lord " (Jer. 23:24).

The omniscience, the omnipresence, and the omnipotence of God are in these ways brought clearly before us. They are contemplated also in that magnificent prayer of David: "Whither shall I go from thy spirit? Or whither shall I flee from thy presence? If I ascend up into heaven, thou art there: if I make my bed in hell, behold, thou art there. If I take the wings of the morning, and dwell in the uttermost parts of the sea; even there shall thy hand lead me, and thy right hand shall hold me" (Ps. 139:7-10).

But we leave aside for the present further comment on all of those important aspects of the doctrine of God. We turn to consider more specifically the knowledge of God. When we do so, we have in view, as we have indicated, the knowledge that God has, first, of himself, and secondly, of reality external to himself. The nature of God's knowledge is determined by the nature of his essence and being. We know that God, by virtue of the fact that he is the Creator of time, exists in a timeless eternal present. That eternal and timeless existence means that there is no succession of passing moments that determines the being of God. It follows that there is similarly no succession of moments that determines his knowledge. God knows himself, we can say, in one single eternal act of knowing.

That is confirmed by his self-designation as the "I am." God did not wait, and in his timeless being he could not wait, for any development or events or awarenesses to provide for him an understanding of himself. God did not wait to discover any aspect of himself or the meaning and character and potential of any of his attributes. If we concluded to the contrary, we should be denying the being of God as we have already understood it. We should thereby reduce God from

Biblical Revelation and the Knowledge of God 61

the level of being to that of becoming. We would then no longer be speaking of the God of the Scriptures.

That realization has implications for what is to be said of the knowledge that God possesses of men and things and of created reality and their histories. Again we must conclude that God knows all things in one eternal act of knowing. In this, of course, lies the essential difference between the what and the how of man's knowledge on the one hand, and God's knowledge on the other.

Man's knowledge is knowledge within, and is structured by, the temporal process that God created and in which he has placed us. God's knowledge, on the other hand, is, for all the reasons implicit in our preceding argument, not temporal at all. God knows all things because he thought all things before the foundation of the world. We can put that differently in terms of all of the facts of reality that exist and are observable.

God knows all of the facts, we say, not in historical sequences and as the outcome of discoveries. He knows all the facts, as he knows himself, in one eternal act of knowing. The facts are what they are because God thought them before the foundation of the world and set them in all of their observable arrangements and constellations. All of the facts are God's facts, and they are what they are because of the place they occupy in God's eternally constructed plan for the history in time of the universe he created. To sum up the meaning of our statement, God does not know as the result of a process of investigation, or as the outcome of a process of discovery on his part. He does not, and could not, wait to discover. He does not hold, therefore, any expectation of possibilities or probabilities as to what might or might not eventuate.

The scriptural data that bear on the point are extensive. "Known unto God are all his works from the beginning of the world," James declared at the council of the church at Jerusalem (Acts 15:18), though variations of reading and textual difficulties do exist at that point of the text.[8] But the truth of the statement turns on the predestinating foreordination of God whereby he "worketh all things after the counsel of his own will" (Eph. 1:11). Somewhat more expansively, the purpose of God, in the predestination, calling, justification, and glorification of his elect, is laid out in the classic Pauline passage that recognizes that all of God's eventuation of the histories of his people is suspended on his foreknowledge and purpose (Rom. 8:28f.).

We distinguish sharply, then, between the nature of God's knowledge and the nature and the process of man's knowledge. We have already made the point by saying that man knows sequentially. We perceive and contemplate and know the objects of our knowledge as they become sequentially available for knowing. We know sequences sequentially. God, too, knows sequences, but he does not know them sequentially. He knows them in a single timeless act of knowing, because, as has been said, he ordered them and ordained them and structured their processes and outcomes. There is, then, no possibility beyond God. Or, from our point of view, we can say that possibility exists for man, but that only that is possible for man which God has already thought and ordained.

We turn in the next chapter to consider the covenants that God has made with man, his fulfillment of the purposes of those covenants, and the manner in which, in doing so, he has communicated the intentions of his purposes to us.

---

[8] See J.A. Alexander, *A Commentary on the Acts of the Apostles* (Edinburgh: Banner of Truth, 1980), vol. 2, 82-83.

Chapter 4

The Covenant-making God

Biblical theology, we have said, is covenant theology. The meaning of that statement and claim will be explored more fully in this chapter. But here as at other parts of our study it is not possible to expand the relevant doctrines at the length they deserve and are accorded in larger treatises. Our objective again is to place before the reader those essentials of doctrine that will contribute to an understanding of their place in the Christian's life and walk.[1]

Four propositions will indicate the essence of what is involved: First, God is a covenant-making and covenant-keeping God; second, because all of God's dealings with man, both before and after the Fall, are covenantal, man is God's covenantal creature and is accordingly under obligation to

---

[1] Herman Witsius, a distinguished seventeenth-century Dutch Reformed theologian, has provided a definitive treatment of this subject in his *The Economy of the Covenants between God and Man*, 2 vols. (Phillipsburg: Presbyterian and Reformed Publishing, 1990). Other discussions are contained in numerous systematic theologies. See also Vickers, *Divine Redemption*, chaps. 2-3 for a discussion of the prelapsarian covenant and the dissent from the covenant of works in contemporary theological literature.

God; third, God's purpose is revealed in successive forms of covenantal administration; and fourth, the Scriptures reveal the parties to, and the objectives and the subjects of, the covenants. It will anticipate what lies ahead to note by way of summary that we shall refer to the covenants as follows:

First, the Covenant of Redemption between the Persons of the Godhead that issued from the council of the Godhead before the foundation of the world and that defined the terms and processes of our redemption.

Second, the covenant of creation that God gave to Adam at his creation, the terms of it and the promises it contained, the obligations and responsibilities it imposed on our first parents, and the extent to which they failed to honor those obligations. Adam was a covenantal person. The meaning of his Fall is that he repudiated the obligations of the covenant under which he stood. That covenant of creation has frequently been referred to as a Covenant of Works, and we shall note the reason for that alternative terminology.

Third, the Covenant of Grace, which established the frame and procedure by which the objectives of the covenant of redemption were to be realized.

Fourth, the covenant of common grace that God established after the terrible development of sin that culminated in his destroying the world in the flood at the time of Noah. In that covenant God promised to preserve the world until his purposes with relation to the church that he would redeem were realized. It follows that God's works of providence are his immanent ordering of all of the events of the history of the world in the interests of the church.

Fifth, the covenants with Abraham and Moses, as they established successive forms of administration of the covenant of grace and the relations that existed between them. When Christ came as the antitype of the types that God established under the preceding forms of administration, he inaugurated what the letter to the Hebrews calls the "new covenant."

The Covenant of Redemption

The covenant of redemption is the outcome of the deliberations of the Persons of the Godhead in the council of redemption before the foundation of the world. It may seem to appear that a contradiction enters at this point when reference is made to the deliberations within the Godhead. For in referring in the preceding chapter to the knowledge of God it was explained that God knew all things in one eternal act of knowing. That knowledge extended to God's awareness of his being, attributes, and purposes, and it excluded any possibility of his sequential acquisition of knowledge. But we recall, as in the previous chapter, that God's revelation to us is necessarily made in anthropomorphic terms, and it is in those terms that we refer to the council of the Godhead. The mystery of the eternal relations between the Persons of the Godhead (the *opera ad intra*) has not been, and by reason of our finitude could not be, disclosed to us. We refer to the council of the Godhead at this point in order to bring into focus the outcome and effect of what God has declared and has ordered in our own historic time for our redemption.

The covenantal design of God that we are now addressing has been referred to frequently as the counsel of God. That terminology has been adopted when the content of the decrees and purposes of God are in view and is consistent with scriptural usage. Ephesians 1:11, for example, states that God works all things according to "the counsel of his own will." Paul states in Acts 20:27 that he had declared "all the counsel of God." Psalm 33:11 says, "The counsel of the Lord standeth forever." The instances could be multiplied. But we refer to the council of the Godhead in order to bring into view what Reformed theologians have recognized in such statements as that of Berkhof, for example, who writes: "The word 'counsel' ... suggests careful deliberation and consultation. It may contain a suggestion of an intercommunication between the persons of the Godhead."[2] It is that intratrinitarian communication that we now contemplate. In that, a distribution of redemptive offices among the Persons of the Godhead occurred and God the Son voluntarily covenanted with the Father and the Holy Spirit to undertake his redemptive mission on our behalf. The fact of that council is clearly stated in the Scriptures.

In his sermon on the day of Pentecost, Peter stated clearly to the Jews that Christ was "delivered by the determinate counsel and foreknowledge of God" (Acts 2:23). Soon thereafter, when the church met in prayer on the occasion of the arrest and subsequent release of Peter and John following their healing of a lame man, their prayer included the recognition that those who crucified our Lord did "whatsoever thy [God's] hand and thy counsel determined before to be done" (Acts 4:28). Then it is in the light of that predeterminate council of the Godhead that Paul could say to the Ephesians that those who are redeemed were "predestinated according to the purpose of him who worketh all things after the counsel of his own will" (Eph. 1:11). Similarly, Paul had said that we were "predestinated ... unto the adoption of children" because God has "chosen us in him before the foundation of the world" (Eph. 1:4). Finally, Peter, in a statement that throws its light on what we shall refer to as the redemptive offices of the Persons of the Godhead, makes the same claim by referring to us as "elect according to the foreknowledge of God the Father, through sanctification of the Spirit, unto obedience and sprinkling of the blood of Jesus Christ" (1 Peter 1:2). Other scriptural statements to the same effect abound, such as Romans 8:29f.: "Whom he [God] did foreknow, he also did predestinate to be conformed to the image of his Son.... Moreover whom he did predestinate, them he also called; and

---

[2] L. Berkhof, *Systematic Theology* (Grand Rapids: Eerdmans, 1939), 103.

whom he called, them he also justified; and whom he justified, them he also glorified."

The parties of the Covenant of Redemption and their respective offices

The parties of the covenant of redemption were the Persons of the Godhead, God the Father, God the Son, and God the Holy Spirit. Their agreement regarding the objectives and the accomplishment of redemption distributed to each of the three Persons what we refer to as redemptive offices. The redemptive office of the Father was that of choosing (as the texts cited above reveal) a certain, definite, and unalterable number of people who, according to his will, were to be redeemed from sin in order to share his eternal glory with him. Those persons whom the Father elected and chose to eternal salvation he gave to the Son to redeem. That is clearly revealed in our Lord's high priestly prayer as we have it recorded in the seventeenth chapter of John's gospel: "Thine they were and thou gavest them me" (John 17:6). Further, his prayer continued at that time, "Holy Father, keep through thine own name those whom thou hast given me" (John 17:11), and "I pray not for the world, but for them which thou hast given me; for they are thine" (John 17:9).

The redemptive office of the Son was to come into the world, to take human nature, yet without sin, into union with his divine nature, to give in that human nature a perfect obedience to the law of God as the substitute for the people whom the Father had given to him to redeem, and to bear the penalty for their sins in his human nature by dying as their substitute. When we come in more detail to the redeeming work of Christ we shall see that what we have just referred to as his redemptive office takes up his active obedience in keeping the law as our substitute, and his passive obedience in his death as our substitute. The redemptive office of the Holy Spirit is to apply to those for whom Christ died the benefits of the redemption that he accomplished. The Holy Spirit confers on them the gifts that Christ purchased for them in his death, notably the gifts of repentance and faith, joy in the Holy Spirit, peace of conscience, and perseverance to the end. The Holy Spirit's office is to call and sanctify those whom Christ has redeemed, to work sovereignly in their lives to conform them progressively to the image of holiness in Christ, and to conduct them to glory. "When he, the Spirit of truth, is come," our Lord said, "he will guide you into all truth.... He shall glorify me; for he shall receive of mine, and shall shew it unto you" (John 16:13-14).

The subjects of the Covenant of Redemption

What, in the light of what has been said, can we say as to the identity of those whom God the Father chose to redeem by the substitutionary work of his Son? Who, in other words, are to be understood as the subjects of the decree to redeem, or those, that is, who are predestined to be the beneficiaries of it? We shall address the same question from another perspective at a later point when we ask, "For whom did Christ die?" At this stage it will be useful to bring the question into perspective by referring to what we call the decrees in terms of which we consider God's redemptive objectives. We can contemplate God's decrees (i) to create, (ii) to permit the Fall, (iii) to elect certain persons to eternal salvation, (iv) to redeem them, and (v) to call and sanctify them. The order in which those decrees have been stated is significant for the understanding of what it is to which they refer. It is to be noted, in particular, that the decree to elect is there stated as being considered after the decree to permit the Fall.

In considering the statement of the decrees of God, two things are worthy of note. First, when we speak of the order of the divine decrees we are not speaking of a temporal order, or a sequential ordering in time. We are speaking, rather, of a logical order, or of the logical relation that exists between the elements of God's decrees, with particular relation to the subjects of them. For the deliberations of the Godhead to which we are now referring took place outside of time, before the creation of time. God himself exists and knows and wills in his timeless eternal day, the comprehension of which is, of course, beyond our created and finite capacity for knowing.

Secondly, by viewing the ordering of the decrees of God as stated above, a conclusion is implied regarding the subjects of the decrees to elect and to redeem. By envisaging the decrees to elect and to redeem after the decree to permit the Fall, we are saying that the subjects of God's redemptive purpose, or the subjects, that is, of the covenant of redemption, were fallen people. It is thereby said that God looked upon all of the fallen offspring of Adam, all of whom were bound in slavery to Satan and sin, and from out of that fallen mass of humanity he freely chose or elected a certain number to redeem. The subjects of the covenant of redemption, then, were, quite simply, fallen people.

It is true that a strong dissent from the doctrine of God's election and predestination is made by some parts of the evangelical church. The origin of that dissent and its recurring expression in the history of the church need not detain us at this point.[3] It is true also that many believers in Christ, who confess with good sincerity that they depend on him alone for their eternal security, nevertheless have difficulty in concurring with this body of doctrine. The explanation, it has to be said, lies in a less than complete understanding of the biblical doctrine of our first parents' fall that brought sin into the world. If the implications of the Fall are recognized, the terrible results of which descended on all people everywhere

---

[3] Discussions of the background to the dissent and its historic claims, in the controversy between Augustine and Pelagius, in the Remonstrant theology that brought forth the response of the Synod of Dordt in the early seventeenth century, and its flowering in latter-day Arminianism and in contemporary evangelicalism, are contained in Vickers, *Divine Redemption*.

by reason of Adam's representation of them as their federal head, it must be seen that we were all by nature in the state of sin that deserved only the judgment of God's wrath and eternal perdition. In the light of that, there was no way in which peace with God and reconciliation with him could be reestablished by any effort that man himself could do or merit that he could earn. It must be left to God himself to design their redemption and provide the way and the means of reconciliation. That he has done in his eternal decree and by setting forth his Son as the sinner's substitute redeemer. The terms in which that was done are precisely what we have inspected as the covenant of redemption. As to the fact that within the terms of that covenant a precisely-defined people were elected to salvation, the cause for wonder is not that God failed to elect everyone, but that in his mercy he elected any. For none deserved his grace and mercy. His honor and his justice would have been vindicated had he left all of Adam's posterity to the eternal perdition their sin warranted. But he had mercy on some. The failure to grasp the meaning of what God has done resolves to a failure to grasp the seriousness of the state of sin, depravity, and inability in which we all existed. The true meaning of sin explains both the necessity and the grace of God's predestinating election. We shall return to the doctrine when we consider the doctrine of man more directly.

The parties and terms of the Covenant of Creation

The parties of the covenant of creation were God on the one hand and our first parents on the other. By the covenant of creation between God and man our first parents were established as covenantal office-bearers in a number of respects. Man as created was to be a prophet, priest, and king. He was to be a prophet in that he was to investigate, understand, interpret, and explain the meaning of the created reality in which he found himself. As a priest he was to dedicate that reality and his understanding of it back to God for his glory. And he was to be a king, in that he was to rule over, or as the text of Genesis says, to "have dominion over," all of reality as God's vicegerent to the glory of God (Gen. 1:28).

At the same time, God established a condition of probation for our first parents. The terms of it are familiar. They were not to eat of the tree of the knowledge of good and evil. But the outcome is all too clear. In their disobedience, they assumed to themselves an autonomy with which they had not been endowed. Involved in that false assumption of autonomy, and resulting from it, was the loss of their created state of holiness. They fell from their initial state, and they did so by repudiating the covenant under which they were bound to obey God. As a result of Adam's sin he was shut out from the initial paradise in which he had first come to consciousness and we, too, participated in his sin. His sin, and more particularly the guilt of his first sin, was imputed to us (Rom. 5:12), so that when he sinned, we sinned.

The Covenant of Grace

What we have discussed as the covenant of creation is frequently referred to in doctrinal theology as the covenant of works. That is because the emphasis of thought then falls more narrowly on the probation under which Adam was placed, the requirement that he should not eat the forbidden fruit, and on the fact, as a result, that if he had continued in a state of obedience his works of obedience would have merited and resulted in eternal life.

But when Adam fell, and when, as a result, he lost his ability to function as prophet, priest, and king, the requirements of the covenant of works were, of course, unfulfilled. We must therefore anticipate at this stage an important point that we shall return to at more length. That is that the honor and the justice of God required that the law which God had given to Adam, and which Adam repudiated, must be kept. Its demands must be met and satisfied. The implication of that is that when Adam fell, the requirements of the covenant of works were in no sense abolished. God's insistence on its demand for man's obedience remained fully in force. Before there could be any eternal life for any of those whom God had created as his image, the full demands of his holy law, as the covenant of works had set it forth, must be met.

But how could that be done? That, if we may speak reverently, was the problem of eternity. There was only one way. It was necessary that the eternal Son of God should come into the world and take human nature into union with his divine nature and in that human nature give the complete obedience to the law that Adam had failed to give. What, then, can we say at this stage as to what it was that Christ accomplished? It is, quite simply, but with profound significance, that Christ fulfilled on our behalf the unfulfilled requirements of the covenant of works. He fulfilled the unfulfilled obligations that we sustained but which, by reason of our sin, we were unable to fulfill for ourselves. Those requirements and obligations had been initially placed on human nature. It was human nature that disobeyed and repudiated the covenant. And it remained necessary, therefore, that God's holy law should be kept and honored in human nature. That is what explains the necessity for the incarnation of Christ. He had to come in human nature in order to be our substitute, both in the keeping of the law and thereby the residual demands of the covenant of works, and in dying for us in order to bear the penalty of our having broken the law.

If the objectives of the covenant of redemption were to be realized, then it was necessary that an arrangement, or a series of arrangements, to accomplish that end must be instituted within the time process in which we existed in the world. For that purpose, what we now refer to as the covenant of grace came into existence. The covenant of grace is to be understood as defining the terms and processes by which the objectives of the covenant of redemption were to be realized.

The parties of the Covenant of Grace

God, the covenant of redemption has declared, elected certain persons to eternal life and gave them to his Son to redeem. To that end God sovereignly entered into a solemn covenant with them, promising to rescue and redeem them and to conduct them to glory. The parties of the covenant of grace, then, were God on the one hand, and those whom he had ordained in Christ to eternal life on the other. Or we can put that in another way, calling on explicit scriptural terms in doing so.

As Paul explained the matter in the first chapter of his letter to the Ephesians, God the Father has chosen us "in Christ," and has "blessed us with all spiritual blessings in heavenly places in Christ" (Eph. 1:3-4). God has always had dealings with his creatures only in Christ. Without pursuing the matter at more length at this point, we can refocus our statement as to the parties of the covenant of grace by saying that they were God on the one hand and us his people as represented by Christ on the other.

The purpose of the covenant of grace was to lead to the realization of the objectives of the covenant of redemption. The former is to be understood as an implementing covenant to achieve the objectives of the latter. But in order to accomplish that, God in his providence worked in and throughout human history to implement successive "forms of administration" of the covenant of grace. We shall see in a moment what those forms of administration were. But first, mention must be made of another intervention by God in human history. It is an aspect of the manner in which, by his works of providence, God exercises his rule over the created reality that he called into existence.

The Covenant of Common Grace

We refer much more briefly at this point to the covenant that God sovereignly set forth at the time of Noah. We are familiar with the respect in which sin had so permeated human history at that time, and the manner in which it had reached such a pervasive perverseness, that God destroyed all human life except that of Noah and his family. But we are interested at this point in what occurred after the flood. God made a covenant with Noah, or, more particularly, we may say that he made a covenant with nature, whereby he promised that he would not again destroy all things in the manner in which he had just done.

In this we have what we refer to as a covenant of common grace because God at that time promised, for a very special and significant reason, to preserve the world and the human race that he had ordained to inhabit it. The objective of God's preservation was that by his subsequent and providential working through human history the world would be preserved until, and in order that, his purposes for the redemption of his chosen people, his church, could be accomplished. Some further aspects of God's covenant of common grace should be noted.

At a minimum, the operations of God's common grace in the world and in history can be considered in both a negative and a positive aspect. Negatively, God's common grace operates in the restraint of sin. By that we mean that man and his culture are not permitted to become as sinful as they could possibly be. In the history of the world and in personal lives, sin is restrained. But the implication follows that in the last day, when the crack of doom has come and when sinners everywhere have come to the full consciousness of their state, common grace will be at an end and sin will realize its full potential and manifestation. In its positive aspect, the common grace of God operates to permit and foster the development of human culture. It is to the common grace of God that advances and developments in the sciences, arts, technologies, and possibilities of human betterment are due.

Consider from that perspective the fact that when our first parents fell into sin and were conscious of their shame that resulted, God made "coats of skin and clothed them" (Gen. 3:21). It has been widely said that in the killing of the animals for that purpose a preindication is given of the necessity for sacrifice and for the substitutionary shedding of blood as an atonement for sin. But are we not to see also in God's action at that point an anticipation of his covenant of common grace? For what was God in effect saying to our first parents in that situation? We recall that the meaning of their sin was that they had made their false and damning assumption of autonomy from God. They assumed that they were sufficient in themselves in all matters of being, knowledge, and behavior. They did not need any criteria that God had established and communicated to them. Now in the sorry state to which they had fallen they continued to assume, it appears, that they could provide for themselves. But their apron of fig leaves was insufficient to meet the necessities of their situation. Did not God act out of grace to tell them, by his providing coats of skin for them, that henceforth he, and not they themselves, would be the source of what they needed to live out their lives in the world as he had established it? Was God's action, then, not a foretaste and an early expression of what would become, in the subsequent and more fully developed human condition and history, the blessings of his common grace?

The forms of administration of the Covenant of Grace

The ways in which God has implemented the covenant of grace in history are revealed in the successive forms of its administration in (i) God's initial covenant with Abraham, (ii) his covenant with his people as given through Moses, and (iii) the inauguration of the "new covenant" in and by Christ. Abraham, Moses, and Christ – the parts they play in the fulfillment of God's purposes of grace illuminate the course of human history and the resolution to which it moves.

The administration of the covenant of grace that was instituted by God's calling of Abraham spans across history from that early time until the coming of Christ. Some 430 years later, as Paul says to the Galatians (Gal. 3:17), God gave the law to Moses and thereby instituted a new form of administration. Important lessons for theological doctrine follow from that history.

First, what Paul stated to the Galatians clarifies the fact that the terms of God's covenant with Abraham were not in any sense altered or abrogated by what was subsequently established at the time of Moses. The covenant with Abraham continued unchanged through the Mosaic administration. When Christ came in fulfillment of the covenantal promise, those to whom God has given the gift of faith and whom he has redeemed and called to himself are actually said to be "Abraham's seed" (Gal. 3:29).

Second, nestling within the covenant with Abraham, that arches through time from Abraham to Christ, is the covenant with Moses. The Mosaic administration extends to the coming of Christ.

Third, Christ came, as our "great high priest" (Heb. 4:14) and as the antitype of all of the types of the Mosaic administration, and his coming was the fulfillment of the initial promise God gave to Abraham. The "new covenant" that Christ inaugurated is, then, the restatement in a new form of administration of the covenant of grace, in terms of which God has sworn to redeem his people and bring them to glory.

The covenant with Abraham

The details of the Abrahamic covenant and the beginnings of its implementation will be familiar and are set out in Genesis 12, 15, and 17. We note within it the threefold elements of God's covenantal promise, the meaning of the covenantal sign, and God's faithful fulfillment of his promise.

The elements of the Abrahamic covenant

God's promise to Abraham was threefold in that he promised him (i) that a great nation would descend from him and that in him, and by means of what God would do through his natural and spiritual descendants, many nations would be blessed; (ii) a land that his descendants would occupy at a precise stage of their history, a promise that was completely fulfilled, as recorded in Joshua 21:43-45: "The Lord God gave unto Israel all the land which he sware to give unto their fathers.... There failed not ought of any good thing which the Lord had spoken unto the house of Israel; all came to pass"; and (iii) that God would be God to the people whom he would make the beneficiaries of the covenantal promises. The culminating and the very precious aspect of God's promise was that he would be God to his people.

In order to establish those covenantal promises in a manner in which they could be understood and grasped and depended upon, God swore an oath of faithfulness. The fact that God swore that oath is recalled by the writer of the letter to the Hebrews, who says that "God, willing more abundantly to show unto the heirs of promise the immutability of his counsel, confirmed it by an oath" (Heb. 6:17). In giving effect to that, God instructed Abraham to take certain animals and, having killed them, to divide them into parts that he was to lay side by side. Then God, in the form of a burning lamp, passed between the divided parts, in a manner that was common in the ratification of covenants at that time in history. The oath that God swore in doing so was an oath of faithfulness to the terms of the covenant. God was saying by that action that if he was not faithful to what he had promised, then let him not be God. He was swearing by his own name. The deeper meaning of that oath-swearing is brought to focus when we pause to take note of an element that was common to all of God's covenantal dealings with man.

The terms of God's covenants with man have always included both a promise of blessing and benefit in the event of obedience to the obligations of the covenant and the promise of curse in the event of disobedience. In other words, there are to be observed in all of the covenant relations the promise of blessing and benediction in the event of obedience, and the promise of curse and malediction in the event of disobedience. God's covenant of creation with Adam clearly involved both the promise of blessing and the promise of curse. If Adam had kept and honored the terms of the covenant he would have merited and gained eternal life. He would have been confirmed in moral righteousness and entered into eternal bliss, the promise of which had been confirmed to him in sacramental terms by the tree of life. But if he disobeyed and repudiated the covenant he would die. The outcome in Adam's case is only too clear.

But it is at that point that the glory of the gospel appears. Two things followed, as we shall see more fully. First, Adam's disobedience and repudiation of his covenantal obligations meant that the promise of malediction must be fulfilled and the curse and the penalty for sin must follow. If that were not so, the justice and honor of God would have been violated. The human condition was thus exposed to the prospect of eternal perdition. Second, the curse of malediction did fall, and it fell with all the weight of the wrath of God. But it fell, not on all individuals, all of whom warranted the curse by reason of their sin, but on the One whom God sent to be the substitute for those whom he had chosen to redeem. When God's people were thus exposed to the curse, they were redeemed because, as Paul wrote to the Galatians, "Christ has redeemed us from the curse of the law, being made a curse for us" (3:13).

The sign and seal of the Abrahamic covenant

The covenantal sign and seal of circumcision that God gave to Abraham (Rom. 4:11) speaks of the deeper implications of the

God-man relation. It projects its significance to the present-day ordinances of the church. The twofold promises inherent in it are reflected again in the church's sacrament of baptism. The facts themselves are recorded in Genesis 17:9ff. It is a complete misconception to imagine that circumcision was, or was ever intended to be, primarily a sign of national identity. Its spiritual significance is paramount. That significance is seen by recalling what has been said about the promise of curse, or the promise of malediction, that was integral to all of God's covenantal arrangements.

First, circumcision was a blood sign. It involved the shedding of blood. By that token it was stating that if the individual, who by the reception of circumcision was recognized as a member of the covenantal community, did not remain faithful to its obligations, then he would be worthy of the death that was prefigured in the shedding of blood that the sign involved.

Second, the covenant sign was therefore a confirmation of the promise of malediction and curse that was integral to the covenant. We can ask whether Abraham and his descendants did, in fact, remain faithful, or whether they merited the curse and the death that the covenant sign portended. We ask, to put it in the simplest of terms, whether Abraham and his descendants sinned. The answer should be clear. "There is none righteous, no not one; all have sinned and come short of the glory of God" (Rom. 3:10, 23). Again we see that the curse was merited and that the curse had to fall. And again we see, as the heart of the gospel states, that the curse fell on Christ as our substitute and redeemer. The great issue of the substitutionary atonement comes to expression and significance at precisely that point.

The covenant with Moses and the Mosaic administration

The Mosaic administration, which extended until the coming of Christ, contained an elaborate system of ceremonial arrangements associated with the tabernacle and later the temple, the sacrificial system, and the priestly phenomena. They formed a temporary or typical and anticipatory order, looking forward to the coming of Christ. The time would come when God would terminate his special relation with his people Israel of old in order that the kingdom of Christ could be established in its widest and most inclusive extent. When Paul said to the Galatians that Christ was "made a curse for us" (Gal. 3:13), he expanded his statement to explain the reasons implicit in God's covenantal intentions. It was in order "that the blessing of Abraham might come on the Gentiles through Jesus Christ" (Gal. 3:14). Christ would come as the antitype of all the types. Then the doors of the kingdom would be thrown wide open to the Gentiles. The anticipations of that, which can be culled from the Old Testament record and from the New, would then be fulfilled. The inclusion of the Gentiles in the kingdom of God was anticipated in the record concerning Melchisedek (Gen. 14:18), Rahab (Jos. 2:3; Heb. 11:31), and Ruth (Ruth 1:16), and in the ministry of our Lord (John 4:7; Matt. 15:22-28). The letter to the Hebrews is an extended exposition of the manner in which Christ came as the perfect high priest and fulfilled all of the promises contained in the types, notably the Levitical priesthood, that had anticipated and pointed to him.

Many aspects of the Mosaic administration anticipated the coming of Christ. Paramount within it, among the many sacrifices that were offered daily and on other special occasions, was the sacrifice made for sin on the annual Day of Atonement (Lev.16). On that day the high priest first offered a sacrifice for his own sin and then, having by that means acquired ceremonial holiness for himself, he offered a sacrifice for the sins of the people. He was permitted and required on that single day of the year to enter the most holy place within the tabernacle and sprinkle the blood of the sacrifice on the Ark of the Covenant and the mercy seat.

But the blood of bulls and goats could not take away sin.

It could not provide a definitive atonement that would deal not only with the ceremonial guilt of the people but with the moral guilt that separated them from God. It was necessary that Christ should come as our "great high priest" to deal with sin by his once-for-all sacrifice. Christ faithfully discharged his earthly high priestly office and he returned to heaven, as the writer to the Hebrews puts it, "for us," and now discharges his heavenly high priesthood on our behalf. In that, "he ever lives to make intercession for us" (Heb. 7:25).

The new covenant in Christ

We shall look in the next chapter at the state of man, both as he was created as the image of God and as he fell into sin. Against the disastrous condition that resulted, the work of redemption that Christ accomplished will appear in its remarkable significance. In that redemptive work Christ brought to its completion and fulfillment God's covenantal promise of blessing. It will complete our preliminary review of God's covenants to recall at this point the promise that he has fulfilled. It is stated in robust terms in the prophecy of Jeremiah: "Behold, the days come, saith the Lord, that I will make a new covenant with the house of Israel, and with the house of Judah ..." (Jer. 31:31ff.). The terms of that covenantal promise as Jeremiah spelled them out are confirmed and applied explicitly to Christ by the writer of the letter to the Hebrews in Hebrews 8:7-13, and again in chapter 10: "This is the covenant that I will make with them after those days, saith the Lord, I will put my laws into their hearts, and in their minds will I write them; and their sins and iniquities will I remember no more" (vv. 16-17).

All of God's covenants are to be understood as sovereign administrations of his grace. His redemptive objectives are complete in Christ who came to declare God unto us (John 1:18) and who, in his coming as "the Lamb of God, which taketh away the sin of the world" (John 1:29), came that "whosoever believeth in him should not perish, but have eternal life" (John 3:15). The song, as a result, that will ring from the lips of his people through all the ages will be: "Thanks be unto God for his unspeakable gift" (2 Cor. 9:15). May our hearts be tuned in thankfulness to praise him.

Chapter 5

Man, Created and Fallen

The biblical doctrine of man addresses a number of questions that project their significance to other levels of Christian belief: What was the original state of man as he came from the hands of his Creator? What does it mean to say that man is the image of God? With what faculties of soul was he endowed, and what was the initial condition of those faculties? What is the meaning of man's fall into sin, and what is the effect of sin on the faculties of the soul? And what is the meaning and implication of the imputation of Adam's sin to all of his posterity?

Contemporary belief regarding the nature and condition of man distances itself from the biblical doctrine and is captive to the thought form of evolutionary anthropology. Man came from the mud, it is imagined, even though his destiny lies with the stars. The story of man, as it is seen from that perspective, is one of a long ascent. It is the story, it is said, of a magnificent journey. As the nineteenth century matured and gave place to the twentieth, the concept of the perfectibility of man was aided and abetted by wider fashions in social and scientific thought that saw its horizons optimistically broadening. But the events of what began as the century of the common man have sobered opinions. The wars of the century, the economic depressions, and the clear collapse of culture and social cohesion have tarnished the earlier optimism. Something is wrong, we have cause to fear, at the very heart of man and his culture. His life is twisted and decaying away from intelligible meaning. His morals have lost what was once their secure moorings, and his social complexes display a seediness and exhaustion.

The real story of man, however, is not one of a long ascent. It is a story of a beginning in a condition of unimaginable bliss, followed by a catastrophic Fall. The story is one of a descent towards the retribution for dereliction from the demands of the covenant that God established with man at his creation. It is true that God has intervened, first at the very beginning in establishing a covenant of grace by which man would be rescued from the entailment of his sin; and secondly, by the administration of his common grace. God's immanent intervention by his common grace has been responsible for the restraint that has inhibited the fuller development of the darkness and depravity of human sin, and it is also responsible for the positive development of scientific progress and human culture.

We observed in the first chapter that man is the image of God. That lies at the basis of our doctrine and influences all of its further development.[1] To recall the definition as we stated it, man is the image of God in that he is created, soul and body, male and female, an immortal, rational, spiritual, moral, and speaking person, capable of reflective self-awareness and purposive action, characterized in his created condition by knowledge and by constitutive holiness and righteousness,

---

[1] The relevant doctrines are discussed in Douglas Vickers, *Christian Confession and the Crackling Thorn: The Imperatives of Faith in an Age of Unbelief* (Grand Rapids: Reformation Heritage Books, 2004), chap. 3, "The Image of God."

and endowed with the capacity for the reception of divine revelation, social relations and communication, and communion with God his Creator. And in the preceding chapter we have seen that when God created man he entered into a covenant with him. We showed that man is a covenantal creature, and that all of God's dealings with him are covenantal dealings. We noted also that man was originally constituted a prophet, priest, and king. His task was to investigate, understand, and explain the meaning of reality, to dedicate that meaning back to God, and to rule over all things to the glory of God. Adam, however, repudiated the obligations of the covenant under which he had been established, and that, in essence, was the meaning of his sin. Sin is always the repudiation of covenantal obligations.

Because man was created as the image of God he came to self-consciousness as the analogue of God. By that we mean that he was like God in every respect in which a personal finite creature can be like his Creator. In his personhood he was revelatory of God. In his condition of derivative personhood he was placed by God in a position of authority over the rest of created reality. He was thereby entrusted with a derivative authority. It was derived from God as his sovereign Creator. It was something bestowed on man and it was not an autonomous authority or a right or prerogative that he had developed, or was capable of developing, from within himself. Man was created with a capacity for knowledge. But what he knows, he knows derivatively. He knows because, in his knowledge capacity as in his being, he is the analogue of God. Again, he was, when he was created, holy, but the holiness by which he was characterized was a derivative holiness. As created, he was immortal. But again, the immortality he possessed was a derivative immortality. We say that man's immortality is derivative because, as Paul stated to Timothy, God "only hath immortality" (1 Tim. 6:16), and he has conferred derivative immortality on man his creature.

We shall examine at more length in this chapter the

meaning of the statements such as these that characterize the state of man, both as created and then as he exists in a state of sin by reason of his Fall.

Man's original state of holiness

When it is said that our first parents as created were holy, it is meant that man as he was created did not exist in some kind of neutral tension, such that tendencies to both good and evil were inherent within him. On the contrary, he was inherently holy, with a natural disposition and inclination to communion with God who walked with him "in the garden in the cool of the day" (Gen. 3:8). God looked on all that he had made and declared that it was good (Gen. 1:31). But differences of view have been held in the history of the church regarding our first parents' initial state. It will be useful to look briefly at a contrary opinion that has gained currency at certain times.

Some theologies, notably that of Roman Catholicism for example, after stating that man in his initial state was holy, proceed to attach a meaning to that term from which it is necessary to dissent. Such theologies go on to claim that man's original holiness was something that was *added* to man after he had been created. The fact that it was something added on (a *donum superadditum*) means that man was not originally characterized by holiness as descriptive of his initial and inherent state and condition. His holiness was in a sense extrinsic, rather than intrinsic. That erroneous doctrine contains other implications.

If such a defective doctrine of man's original condition is held, it inevitably points also to a defective doctrine of sin and of man's fall into the state of sin. For the error we have just identified implies that when man fell, all that happened was that he lost the gift of holiness that had previously been given to him. He was thereby reduced again to the state in which he existed before the gift of holiness had been given to him in the first place. That means, in turn, that man in sin possesses not only the faculties of soul, but also the capacities and abilities of those faculties, that he had as he was originally created. But the Scriptures require us to hold, to the contrary, a much more radical and far reaching explanation of sin. Sin, it is to be insisted, affected the faculties of the soul in a much more radical way than is contemplated by such an erroneous doctrine of man's creation.

Man is the image of God

To say that man *is* the image of God is to make a very different claim from the statement that man *bears* the image of God. Man does not simply bear the image of God in the sense, in one way or another, that the image of God has been impressed upon him. Rather, man *is* the image of God, and that in several important respects.

First, he is immortal. The Scriptures state that God "breathed into man the breath of life, and man became a living soul" (Gen. 2:7). It is not true or sufficient to say that man *has* a soul, and that he *has* a body. What is to be said is that man *is* both body and soul. When we say that man is soul, we are saying that he is *spiritual*. He possesses the capacity for communication with God and with others of God's created rational beings. The nature of the soul that man is, is such that he is a derivative analogue of God. He has, as we have said, derivative immortality. Because he is what he is, he will necessarily live for ever. The reality, however, is that now, as a result of the entrance of sin, that immortality will be lived out for ever in a state of eternal separation from God or, in the case of those whom God has redeemed, in the presence of God in Christ for ever.

Second, man is rational. He possesses the faculty of thought and imagination and reflective self-awareness. Man thinks, because God thinks. He can understand because God has implanted within him the faculty of soul that is capable of investigating the meaning and explanation of things. He is endowed with a facility of seeing things in their ordered or their logical relations. He is capable of seeing that the logical relations existing between things are the reflection of the order, and of the laws of order, in which God has structured created reality. That, of course, is why it is to be said that the laws of logic are the same for the Christian and the non-Christian person. They have been createdly impressed on the human consciousness. The difference between the use that the Christian and the non-Christian make of those laws of thinking is due to the manner in which the fall into sin has affected the very foundational assumptions or presuppositions of thought. In the case of the unbeliever, a terrible bias has been introduced to the soul. A sharpness of intellect will accomplish nothing of significance if it runs in a biased fashion on an irrelevant track. The laws of right thinking are not something of human invention. Logic is a divine endowment.

Third, man is the image of God in that he speaks. The fact that he alone of all God's creatures speaks is, perhaps, the highest respect in which, in his original constitution, he is the image of God. For man was created a speaking person for two reasons. First, he speaks in order that he can understand the meaning of God's speech to him. And secondly, he speaks in order that he can speak back to God the meaning that he discovers in reality and that he can enjoy communion with God.

Fourth, man is the image of God in that he is a moral person. He is capable of judgments between right and wrong behavior and action. He sustains, moreover, a responsibility for decisions and choices of action, and he is accountable to God for the manner in which he discharges his moral responsibility in relation to the law of God. A different way of making that statement is to say that man will be, in his behavior and manner of life, either righteous in his relation to the law of God or he will live and act unrighteously. In an earlier context, when the attributes of God were contemplated, the fact that God has revealed himself as a moral being was recognized in the fact that all of his actions, thoughts, and ordinations are consistent with the eternal holiness in which he exists. God is himself righteous in that in all of his government of the world that he made he is consistent with the law of his own holy being. But he is not, and he could not be, subject to a law that is, or could be, higher than and external to himself. If the latter were true, he would not be the God who has revealed himself in the Scriptures.

While we have not yet spoken explicitly of the meaning of sin, an implication of what we have just said is that it would be an error to say that when he sinned man lost the image of God. For in the first place, we have said not that man at first *had* or *bore* the image of God, but that he *is* the image of God. Then secondly, man as he now exists in his sinful and unregenerate state is still the image of God, in that he is still an immortal, rational, spiritual, moral, and speaking person. That is clearly stated, for example, in what God said to Noah immediately after the flood. The reason why, at that time, capital punishment was instituted for murder was that man, God said, is "the image of God" (Gen. 9:6). Again, we have it in the book of James that man as he exists, and against whom we are frequently too ready to speak evil, was "made after the similitude [or likeness or image] of God" (James 3:9).

The faculties of soul and their initial status

Two questions are now raised by the biblical doctrine of man. When we consider the faculties of the soul our thought should be organized to contemplate, first, the capacities and order of the faculties as they existed before our first parents' fall; and second, the respects in which the faculties were affected by sin. We take the first question first. In doing so, our focus falls on the nature and capacities of the faculties as first, the mind or the intellectual faculty; second, the heart or the emotional faculty; third, the will or the volitional faculty; and fourth, the conscience or the judicial faculty.

Much has been made in the history of doctrine of the possible defects and deficiencies of what might appear at this point as a so-called "faculty psychology." The eighteenth-century American theologian, Jonathan Edwards, has remarked judiciously on the subject of the faculties in his treatise on the will. He rejects what had become referred to as the "scholastic faculty psychology." But he did so in the sense that he rejected the notion of the autonomous, uninstructed activity of the faculties separately considered. For Edwards, to take his prime example, the actions and decisions of the will were such that "every act of the will is some way connected with the understanding, and is as the greatest apparent good is," and "it is impossible for the will to choose contrary to its own preponderating inclination."[2] In the same way it will be observed in what follows that the order of relation and the interdependencies among the human faculties must be accorded appropriate recognition.

From that perspective, two things are to be said about the faculties of the soul as they existed in man before the Fall. First, a harmony among the faculties existed; and second, the mind, or the intellectual faculty, was the prince of the faculties of the soul. That is so because, as we have seen, God created man as the image of himself in order that he could have communication with him. Man understood God when God walked with him in the garden in the cool of the day (Gen. 3:8). With the mind man had a clear understanding of what God communicated to him regarding his laws and mandates and the requirements of man's probation. We can say that with the mind man naturally knew God in an uncluttered though finite way, and he knew what he knew because it was communicated to him by God's gracious revelation. We saw in a previous chapter that God gave to man a partial

---

[2] Jonathan Edwards, *The Freedom of the Will* (Morgan, PA.: Soli Deo Gloria Publications, 1996), 86, 73. See also Douglas Vickers, *Christian Confession and the Crackling Thorn*, 59-60.

revelation of himself, and while man's finitude precluded him from a comprehensive knowledge of God, he could and he did in his initial state have a true knowledge of God.

As with the mind man naturally knew God, so with his heart, or his emotional faculty, he naturally loved God and sought after the things of God. That follows from what we have already said regarding the fact that man in his original constitution was holy. He was, in the respects we have indicated, a finite analogue of God. The reality of our first parents' situation, then, was that because with the mind they naturally knew God, and with the heart they naturally loved God, the mind and the heart together were able to instruct the will to obey God. Moreover, in man as created there was no disturbance of conscience, and man knew and judged correctly what his pristine relation to God his Creator was and what the law of God required of him. In that condition, he enjoyed the calmness and serenity of conscience in the awareness that he was like God.

The entrance of sin and the effect on the faculties of the soul

We shall characterize in a moment what was involved in the act of sin that our first parents committed. But we maintain for the present our focus on the faculties of the soul and contemplate the effects of sin upon them. It can be said immediately that two things correspond to, or reflect the reversal of, the state of the faculties as we have just looked at them in man before he fell. First, at the Fall the harmony of the faculties was shattered; and second, the mind or the intellectual faculty surrendered its hegemony and lost its place as the prince of the faculties of the soul. After the Fall, and as a result of the Fall, the heart or the emotional faculty now lords it over the mind. Man now does what he wants to do, not because he knows with the mind that it is right, but because the passions of the heart propel his actions. Of course there exists, by virtue of the common grace of God, certain restraints on human action. Man is not as sinful as he is capable of being. God's common grace operates in human history, negatively as a restraint against sin, and positively as a means of permitting the development of science and human culture.

Again, people do act in such a way as to preserve, in one way or another, cultural proprieties. We say that sinful man is capable of civic good. But while that is so, two further things are to be said of him. First, and apart from the regenerate person's appeal to the Word of God, the categories or the criteria that determine his action are the criteria that he dreams up for himself apart from what God has decreed for his guidance; and second, while the sinner is capable of such civic good, and while he is capable of making meaningful contributions to the development of human culture, he is, as the Scriptures make clear, totally incapable of any good that has eternal value.

The state of the faculties of the soul in man's sinful condition, that of darkness and the ignorance of God into which he fell, is clearly explained in the Scriptures. Paul explained the state of the sinful mind to the Corinthians by saying that "the god of this world [Satan] has blinded the minds of them which believe not" (2 Cor. 4:4). And the only reason why any person knows God is because "God, who commanded the light to shine out of darkness [at the original creation] has shined in our hearts, to give the light of the knowledge of the glory of God in the face of Jesus Christ" (2 Cor. 4:6). The apostle had said also that "the natural man receiveth not the things of the Spirit of God. For they are foolishness unto him. Neither can he know them, because they are spiritually discerned" (1 Cor. 2:14).

As to the state of the heart, the condition of fallen man is as it was described at an earlier point of human history. Genesis 6:5 says that "the wickedness of man was great in the earth, and every imagination of the thoughts of his heart was only evil continually." That condition was sadly all too apparent again when the earth was replenished after the Noahic flood. It gave rise to the repeated complaint of God against his own people, such that the prophet Jeremiah characterized the condition by stating that "the heart of man is deceitful above all things, and desperately wicked. Who can know it?" (Jer. 17:9).

As to the will, the condition of fallen man in bondage to Satan and sin is all too clear from only a minimal look at the Scriptures. Our Lord on one occasion stated to the Jews that they were in a state of bondage. They remonstrated with him and forcibly rejected his claim. They were, they said, "Abraham's seed, and were never in bondage to any man." But our Lord spoke of their bondage to sin. The will was not free. It was bound. Christ explained more fully: "Whosoever commits sin is the slave of sin." Moreover, he said to the Jews, "Ye are of your father the devil, and the lusts of your father ye will do" (John 8:33-44). Sadly, one of the most serious implications of Adam's Fall is that in the Fall man lost his free will. Now he is the slave and the dupe of the Devil.

An expressive explanation of the unregenerate person's bondage to sin, and of the resulting inability and bondage of will, is contained in our Lord's response to the Jews when they accused him of casting out devils by the power of Beelzebub, the prince of devils. To the contrary, he claimed, he cast out devils by "the finger of God." Moreover, he explained the condition of those who were bound in sin by saying, "When a strong man armed [Satan] keepeth his palace, his goods are in peace. But when a stronger than he [Christ] shall come upon him, he taketh from him all his armour wherein he trusted, and divideth the spoils" (Luke 11:19-22). The inescapable fact is that man in his sinful state is the peaceful dupe and slave of the devil. That is the measure of the sorry state to which sin has reduced him. It is only by the sovereign grace of God that anyone is rescued from that state and brought to salvation in Christ. We shall see more fully in a later chapter the work of the Holy Spirit in regeneration that renews the fallen soul and turns the sinner to reconciliation with God in Christ.

Paul has given us the same explanation of the natural sinful condition. He speaks at length in the sixth chapter of his letter to the Romans of the unregenerate person's slavery to Satan and sin. Don't you know, he says in effect, that you are the slaves of those whom you choose to obey, "whether of sin unto death, or of obedience unto righteousness" (Rom. 6:16). The contrary case is then portrayed. "But God be thanked," Paul says, "ye were the servants of sin, but ye obeyed [that is the will in action] from the heart [that is the emotional faculty in action] that form of doctrine which was delivered you" [that is the mind in action] (Rom. 6:17). In Paul's delineation there we have the activity of the faculties of the soul in the movement of the individual from the state of darkness, slavery, and sin into the light of the grace of God. The mind is engaged in the embrace of the doctrines of God's revelation, the heart is engaged in concurrence with the truth of the doctrines that are then apprehended, and the will is moved to obey the call of God to rescue and relief in Christ.

The meaning of sin and the nature of Adam's first sin

A number of questions that must now be addressed clarify the radical meaning of sin and the state of sin into which we have fallen. We say that Adam's Fall was an ethical lapse and not a metaphysical lapse, a lapse on the level of behavior and not on that of being. But why is that so? Why, following that lapse, is sin essentially and primarily a matter of a state in which we exist, since the Fall and by nature and as a result of the Fall? What is the relation of sin to the holiness of God? What is the relation between sin and law, notably the law of God? What do we mean by the imputation of Adam's sin to his posterity? How do we characterize more precisely the sin that Adam committed? Why do we speak of the self-direction of sin?

The Fall an ethical lapse

We make the statement that sin is an ethical lapse for two reasons. First, by virtue of the constitution of his faculties of soul, man as created was the image of God. And in the light of that, as he now exists in the state of sin as a result of the Fall he is still the image of God. The implication of that is that the person as he now exists is the same being, with the same faculties, the same individuality and responsibility, that he was before he fell. The faculties were affected by the entrance of sin in the way we have seen, and certain disabilities of soul resulted. The mind was darkened and rendered ignorant of the things of God, the heart was turned away from God and men became, as Paul explained to the Romans, "haters of God" (Rom. 1:30), the will was enslaved, and the conscience was seared and dulled. But while that is so, the individual person remained God's created and responsible being, and his obligations to God in terms of the covenant that God first established with him remain.

When we say that the Fall was an ethical lapse, then, we are saying that man continues to be responsibly man, and that the action by which he fell was simply that he did something that he should not have done. The Fall, that is, was a matter of a defective action, a matter of wrong behavior. The Fall resulted, in that manner, from a certain action of the faculties of the soul, not from any change in the intrinsic nature of the faculties of the soul.

The second reason for stating that the Fall was an ethical lapse, a lapse on the level of behavior and not of being, is that now, after he has fallen, man remains under obligation to God and to the law of righteousness that God has established. All of this is again contrary to the theology that explains the fall by saying that when man fell he descended to a lower level in the chain of being. Such an error in theological doctrine follows from the false philosophic assumption that God and man both exist in one continuous chain of being. Such a claim denies what the Scriptures insist upon, namely the Creator-creature distinction. It is not true to say that there exists a commonness of being in which God and man both share. God is transcendentally God, separate from and above all else, and all that exists external to the Godhead has its being because God spoke it into existence. That is why we said at the beginning that man, being separate from God, is an analogue of God. But he does not share in being with God. Man has his being derivatively from God, and he remains in his personhood responsible to God.

But of the fact of the Fall and of sin there is no doubt. We have it in the sacred record that when our first parents sinned, when they terminated their probation by eating of the forbidden fruit, God drove them out from the garden, and drove them out from communion with himself. He placed the cherubim to guard the entrance to the tree of life, lest our parents should sin further by endeavoring to partake of that tree, thinking thereby to achieve a direct entrance to life that was forbidden to them. God, in an act of grace, preserved them from that sin by barring their way to the tree of life.

The entrance of sin implied that at the Fall man suffered both a *deprivation* and a *depravation*. In answer to the question, "wherein consists the sinfulness of that estate whereinto man fell," the Westminster Shorter Catechism states, "the sinfulness of that estate … consists in the guilt of Adam's first sin, the want of original righteousness, and the corruption of his whole nature."[3] The *deprivation* consisted in the "want of original righteousness," and the *depravation* consisted in the "corruption of his whole nature."

By the entrance of sin, man was completely undone. His state of original holiness and righteousness was lost, connoting his deprivation, and his whole nature was corrupted, reflecting his depravation. Now he was depraved in all of the faculties of his soul. Now he had lost communion with God

[3] Westminster Shorter Catechism, Question 18.

and he stood, instead, under the wrath and the curse of God. Now he was liable to all of the miseries of this life that were entailed upon the entrance of sin, and he stood subject to the prospect of eternal perdition for his sin. His condition was indeed a sorry one. There could be no alleviation and no escape from the penalty of his sin unless God should intervene and provide a way of redemption.

Sin, holiness, and the law of God

It is clearly stated in the first epistle of John that "sin is the transgression of the law" of God (1 John 3:4). That is another way of saying that sin is an ethical lapse. It is a matter of wrong action in relation to law. It follows from what has been said that while that is so, it is necessary to distinguish between the actions of sin and the state and condition of sin into which we have fallen and from which the sinful action emanates. While sin is, then, wrong action, the radical reality is that we exist in a state of sin. That is the root explanation of our fallen condition. We should note what that implies.

First, sin is sin because it has outraged the holiness of God. That is what is involved in saying that sin is the transgression of the law. We must look, not only to the law of God for what it is in itself, and to the act of transgression of it to which the sinner's conscience alerts him. We must look to the deeper fact that the law of God is what it is because it is a reflection of the holiness of God himself. When we sin against God's law, we are offending the holiness of God.

Second, it is because sin is an offense to the holiness of God that the wrath of God is displayed against sin. It may not be popular at the present time to speak of the wrath of God. But the Scriptures have elevated the reality of God's wrath against sin and the sinner to explain the deepest meaning of sin itself. To consider only one statement of the case, the apostle John clarified that very fact in his first epistle when he explained the meaning and compass of the love of God. We have there the statement that "God sent his Son to be the propitiation for our sins." "Propitiation" means "setting at peace." And it is involved in the Scriptural statement at that point that God is set at peace with us because Christ, in his substitutionary death, has satisfied the demands of his wrath against us. But why, it must be asked, was God's attitude to us in our state of sin one of wrath? It was because, as we have said, our sin was an outrage to his holiness.

God, the revelation of his word makes clear, hates sin. He abhors sin. The prophet Habakkuk has told us that God "is of purer eyes than to look upon evil" (Hab. 1:13); and because of that the wrath of God is directed, justly and irrevocably, against the sinner and his sin. The wrath of God is directed to the sinner irrevocably, that is, unless the grace and mercy of God intervene and by his Spirit he imparts to the sinner the gift of repentance and turns him to Christ. God hates the very beginnings of sin in the hearts and imaginations of his creatures. The prophet Zechariah observed, "Let none of you imagine evil in your hearts.... For all these are things that I hate, saith the Lord" (Zech. 8:17). The same statement of God's revulsion against sin can be observed in Isaiah 1:14, Isaiah 63:10, Jeremiah 44:4, and Ezekiel 16:43, among many other passages. The Psalmist has summed it up in his address to God by saying, "Thou hatest all workers of iniquity" (Ps. 5:5).

Charnock, again, has in similar terms an insightful understanding of sin, the glory of God, and the relation between them. The "love of holiness," Charnock observes, "cannot be without a hatred of everything that is contrary to it." And in the same context he traces out the implications of God's self-love. "As God necessarily loves himself, so he must necessarily hate everything that is against himself; and as he loves himself for his own excellency and holiness, he must necessarily detest whatever is repugnant to his holiness, because of the evil of it. Since he is infinitely good, he cannot but love goodness, as it is a resemblance to himself; and cannot but abhor unrighteousness as being most distant from him, and contrary to him. If he have any esteem for his own perfections, he must needs have an implacable aversion to all that is so repugnant to him, that would, if it were possible, destroy him, and is a point directed not only against his glory, but against his life. If he did not hate it, he would hate himself; for since righteousness is his image, and sin would deface his image, if he did not love his image, and loathe what is against his image, he would loathe himself, he would be an enemy to his own nature."[4]

The imputation of Adam's sin

The meaning of sin is not exhausted until it is acknowledged that, and why, we who are descended from Adam are in ourselves sinful. It is all too clear that the disabilities of the state of sin cling to us. We are disabled from our very birth, conceived in sin, as the Psalmist has lamented (Ps. 51:5), and subject to the condemnation that "there is none righteous ... all have sinned and come short of the glory of God" (Rom. 3:10, 23). Of the fact that we come into this world in, and with, a sinful nature, there can be no doubt. The doctrinal explanation why that is so has been stated quite straightforwardly by the Westminster Shorter Catechism when it says, "The covenant being made with Adam, not only for himself but for his posterity, all mankind descending from him by ordinary generation sinned in him and fell with him in his first transgression."[5] The guilt of Adam's first sin was imputed to us all.

The short answer to our question, then, is that when Adam sinned, we sinned. That is made clear in the tightly reasoned argument that Paul presents in the fifth chapter of his letter to the Romans (Rom. 5:12ff.). God had established

---

[4] Charnock, *The Existence and Attributes of God*, 455.
[5] Westminster Shorter Catechism, Question 16.

Adam as our federal head. He was our representative, and the reality of our situation is that his sin, and particularly the guilt of his sin, is imputed to us. That guilt is placed to our account. It is regarded as our sin and guilt. And as a result, it is by Adam's sin that we are constituted sinners. The matter of imputation stands as one of the profoundest aspects of the entire meaning of our position. For as will be seen, in the same way as God imputed Adam's sin to us, or placed the guilt of his sin to our account and reckoned it as our sin, so he has imputed the righteousness of Christ to those for whom Christ died. The righteousness of Christ is in a similar way placed to their account, and by the grace of God it is reckoned as their righteousness. That imputation of the righteousness of Christ to the sinner was possible by virtue of the imputation of the guilt of the sinner's sin to Christ. We shall return to the relevant doctrines.

In the history of theology there has been a good deal of debate, and even serious misunderstanding, as to the meaning of the imputation of Adam's sin. The question has arisen as to the manner in which we should understand the guilt of Adam's sin to have been imputed to us. In more technical terms the question has been argued as to whether the sin in view was imputed to us *mediately* or *immediately*. In other words, when it is agreed that the guilt of Adam's first sin was placed to our account, should we say that we hold, then, a doctrine of *mediate imputation* or a doctrine of *immediate imputation?* The difference between those alternative views has to do with what might or might not have been the ground on which God has made the imputation of sin to us, or the ground upon which we were made sinners by Adam's Fall.

Take, first, the possibility of mediate imputation. The very terms in which that doctrine is stated suggest that something exists, some basis or principle or reason, that provides the ground of imputation. Something, that is, mediates between God's decision to impute sin and the actual placing of it to our account. What that something is has frequently been understood to be our fallen nature. Our fallen nature, it is said, is inherited from Adam. And because we inherit that fallen nature, it carries along with it the reality of sin, the guilt of which is thereby imputed to us. On that view the ground or basis of the imputation of sin is our fallen nature.

There can be no argument that we come into this world with a fallen nature. The question to be addressed, however, is whether we can be said to be sinners because we come into the world with a fallen nature. The answer we give is in the negative. It is not the case that we are sinners because we come into the world with a fallen nature. The precise contrary is true. The reality is that we come into the world with a fallen nature because we were constituted sinners by Adam's Fall. And whatever is to be said from that point on, the implication is not that we are sinners because we sin, but that we sin because are sinners. We have been constituted sinners. That state and condition resulted from the imputation to us of the guilt of Adam's first sin.

The doctrine of mediate imputation, then, is to be rejected. We hold, on the contrary, to a doctrine of *immediate imputation*. The use of the word "immediate" does not have reference to time, in the sense that guilt was imputed to us immediately when Adam sinned. That is, of course, true. But what is being said at this point is that the imputation of sin was immediate in the sense that there was no other mediating cause, or no other intermediating ground, that provided the basis for God's imputation. In the mysterious purpose and providence of God, because he had established Adam as our federal and representative head, when Adam sinned, all of the race that was to be descended from him by ordinary generation (thus excepting the incarnate Son of God) sinned in and with him. As Paul put it bluntly in his letter to the Romans, when Adam sinned, we sinned.

The nature of Adam's sin

Adam's sin was essentially his repudiation of his covenantal obligations. Those obligations required him to acknowledge that he was the derivative analogue of God, that the knowledge he possessed was derivative knowledge, his holiness was derivative holiness, and that the task mandated to him was that he should rule in and over this world as the vicegerent of God. But the essence of Adam's sin was that, contrary to the demands of those obligations, he asserted his autonomy from God. From the perspective of Adam's first sin, and from the perspective of what it means for all individuals since, what we have just said strikes to the heart of the meaning of sin. Sin, then, is always the assertion of autonomy from God.

Of course, Adam's assertion of autonomy was a false assertion. The fact that it was false constitutes its sinfulness. But we must see at least briefly what it was and what it entailed. Adam's false assertion of autonomy came to expression on three levels. It involved the assertion of metaphysical, epistemological, and ethical autonomy. We would not raise those technical terms if it was not so seriously important to get at the root of the meaning of sin. Let us look at them a little more fully.

First, metaphysics is that branch of knowledge that has to do with the theory of being, and the assertion of metaphysical autonomy means that as to his being, Adam asserted that he was independent of God. He was not prepared to acknowledge God as his Creator who rightly and justly required obedience from him. In a profound and sorry sense, in his Fall Adam denied his creaturehood.

Second, the assertion of epistemological autonomy means that Adam asserted that he was not dependent on God for all that he knew and for his capacity for knowledge. Epistemology is that branch of thought that has to do with the origin, processes, and validity of knowledge. It has to do with the criteria in terms of which the truth of claims to knowledge can be established. The Devil told Adam that what God had said was not necessarily true. The reality of the situation in which Adam had placed himself was that he then assumed he was faced with two contrasting options as to knowledge. God said one thing, and the Devil said another. What was Adam to believe and act upon? He decided that he would make his own decision, independently of the forces bearing upon him. For he was, he now asserted, autonomous. He would not be bound by what either God or Satan had said. He would decide for himself. That is the assertion of epistemological autonomy. It meant for Adam, and it means the same thing for us all as fallen individuals, that he could find within himself, or perhaps he could deduce from the world around him, all of the necessary criteria of knowledge. In making that assertion of autonomy, Adam had already fallen from his initial covenantal status, and he had by that very fact already placed himself under the power of Satan and had fled from God.

Third, because Adam asserted that he was independent of God on the levels of both being or creaturehood, and of knowledge, it followed that the position he took involved also the false assertion of ethical autonomy. By that claim, he asserted that he did not need to take his criteria of proper and morally correct behavior from God and from the law that God had set forth. He could, he asserted, find all necessary criteria of behavior within himself, or again within the world around him. On that level again, Adam asserted his independence from God.

That continues to be the meaning of sin in the lives of all those descending from Adam by, as the catechism states, ordinary generation. Sin means, in essence, the assertion that we are independent of God. We are, to the extent that we are trapped in sin, stating that we are, and that we can successfully be, a law unto ourselves.

The self-direction of sin

All that we have said as to the meaning of sin leads to a final statement regarding its character. We refer now to what can be called the *self-direction of sin*. As sin takes hold of a person, the passions and the energies of his soul are directed, no longer towards his Creator to whom he has sustained covenantal obligations, but towards himself.

In Adam's state of innocence the faculties of his soul were such that he naturally loved God, he loved the communicated law of God, he enjoyed communion with God, and he directed his life, short though it may have been before the Fall, to pleasing God. In his initial state in Paradise, man existed in a condition of knowledge, righteousness, and holiness (Eph. 4:24; Col. 3:10). With the mind he knew God and knew the will of God, and he had a true apprehension of the perfections of God. He had, also, a true knowledge of the conditions of his own existence and of what, in accordance with the benefits, obligations, and promises of the creation mandate, God required of him. And under the impulse of his pristine mind and heart, with his will in his unfallen state he naturally served God.

But we have observed the implications for the faculties of the soul of the state into which man fell. The state of sin is such that the energies and passions and faculties of the soul are directed against God. The harmony of the faculties is shattered to the extent that now the heart rather than the mind has assumed hegemony in the soul. Now, in a sadly perverse sense, the heart is the prince of the faculties.

That, in shortest compass, is the meaning of sin and the state of man in sin. It means that in his unregenerate state he no longer does what he does because a mind that reflects the holy character of God instructs him. Now he does what he wants to do. The passions, the heart, the desires are in command. That is the explanation of the disordered disruption of the human condition. There is no restraint now, apart from those external restraints of conduct that civilization, due to the common grace of God, establishes. Reason has capitulated to passion in the human condition. There is no longer a holy law before the minds of men. Ignorance, guilt, and misery disguise their seductions and pretenses and degrade men's souls. Only the rescue and relief that Christ our Redeemer has provided can meet the sorry case.

When we speak, then, of the self-direction of sin we mean that now, in the state of sin, man's essential and his primarily motivating love of self has replaced his love of God. He has now become a god unto himself. Or in other terms, he has made gods for himself in his own image, gods that he has found within the world of reality that he should have dedicated to the glory of the true God. Or he has manufactured his idols from within his own distorted and alienated imagination. The love of self, in this all-determining way, has displaced the primeval love of God. Man in sin, in short, in a sadly comprehensive and all-determining sense, is a law unto himself.

But against all that the gospel of grace rings clear. In the covenant of grace God has set forth a redemption for sinners. We turn in the next chapter to consider the Person of Christ whom God has sent to rescue his people from the entailment of their sin.

Chapter 6

The Person of Christ

At the beginning of his first epistle the apostle John makes two statements that strike to the heart of the meaning of the gospel. "God," he says, "is light, and in him is no darkness at all." God, it is being said, is a holy God. It is with an eternally holy God that we have to do, and it is such a God who has redeemed us to himself. That he did by sending his Son into the world. And of Christ who came, John says, "The blood of Jesus Christ his Son cleanseth us from all sin" (1 John 1:5, 7). That statement brings clearly before us the fact that it is on what was accomplished by and through the shedding of the blood of Christ that our entire redemption depends. It is the blood of Christ that brings us, through the faith that by his Spirit he creates within us, to God the Father. John is here stating that all of our salvation, in all of its parts and in all of its scope and prospect, is what it is because the blood of Christ was shed on our behalf. The statement accords with that of Paul to Timothy, "Christ Jesus came into the world to save sinners" (1 Tim. 1:15).

The gospel holds that twofold statement at its core. First, when God's people languished in the condition of sin, the eternal God took the initiative and designed a means of rescue and reconciliation for them. Second, that initiative involved nothing less than the humiliation and the death of the eternal Son of God who paid the substitute penalty for the sins of his people. The hymn writer, John Henry Newman, has captured the gospel in a stanza: "O loving wisdom of our God!/ When all was sin and shame,/ A second Adam to the fight/ And to the rescue came."[1] That remarkable design and accomplishment calls for brief review. In this and the following chapter we consider what is to be said, first, of the Person of Christ the redeemer, and secondly, of the nature of the redemptive work he accomplished.

A number of propositions set the relevant issues in order. First, as was seen in an earlier chapter, God is not only transcendent in his eternal being, he is immanently active in the world and its history. Second, God acts immanently in the world in the Persons of his Son and his Holy Spirit. Third, the most remarkable mystery of God's action is that he who created time entered into time in the Person of his Son. Fourth, Jesus Christ, the incarnate Son of God who entered into the world to be our redeemer, was not a human person. He was, and he remained, a divine Person. And fifth, the incarnation of the Son of God was the only way in which redemption could be accomplished. Cecil Francis Alexander saw that clearly when he wrote, "There was no other good enough to pay the price of sin;/ he only could unlock the gate of heav'n and let us in."[2]

We ask two questions. Who is Jesus Christ? And what is the significance of his coming and the work he came to do? Who was it who walked in this world as a man, who suffered and learned obedience in his human nature, and who died as

---

[1] John Henry Newman, "Praise to the Holiest in the height ..." in *Congregational Praise* (London: Independent Press for the Congregational Union of England and Wales, 1951) and various hymnals.

[2] Cecil Francis Alexander, "There is a green hill far away ..." in *Trinity Hymnal* (Atlanta: Great Commissions Publications, 1990) and various hymnals.

the substitutionary sacrifice for sin in his human nature? We ask that question because all of the doctrines of Christianity center for their meaning on the Person of Christ. It is not simply the *teaching* of Christ that provides the foundation and establishes the superstructure of Christianity. It is rather the *Person* of Christ. That distinguishes Christianity from all other systems of thought. Take away the founders of the other systems, and the structure of thought may remain. We may have Kantian philosophy without Kant, Arminianism as a system of theology without Arminius. That is because their significance centers in what they taught, not in what they were. But that is not so with Christianity. Christianity is what it is because in his Person Christ is who he is.

At the very foundation of our doctrine we are confronted with the incarnate Christ. Who was this Person who walked the roads of Galilee, doing good, healing the sick and the lame, raising the dead, and preaching repentance and the kingdom of God? This, the revelation of God tells us, was none other than the Son of God, the second Person of the Godhead. The Son of God became man for men, that a redemption from sin might be provided for the sinners whom God had chosen to redeem. Well has Charles Wesley said in his hymn, "Veiled in flesh the Godhead see;/ Hail th'incarnate Deity."[3] How, then, is human thought to evaluate the One who was God and man?

The incarnation of Christ in historical time

No more profound mystery exists than that of the incarnation of the Son of God. If there is any point at which we stand in awe and wonder and amazement at the "mystery of godliness" (1 Tim. 3:16), surely it is here. At this point we "see through a glass darkly," we "know in part," and we hold to the hope of

---

[3] Charles Wesley, "Hark! The herald angels sing ..." in idem and various hymnals.

the fuller revelation that is yet to come (1 Cor. 13:12). The apostle John has made it clear that here we confront the very touchstone of Christian confession. "Every spirit that confesseth that Jesus Christ is come in the flesh is of God" (1 John 4:2). We know that the Word, who was with God and was God "was made flesh and dwelt among us ... full of grace and truth" (John 1:1, 14).

The fact and the doctrine of the incarnation stand at the very beginning of Christian doctrine. We recognize that in coming into the world the second Person of the Godhead entered into the time that he had made. In his doing so, the eternal and the temporal are brought into a new relation, but without the rupture that would have occurred if the eternal and the temporal had become commingled and confused. The process of redemption, therefore, was actually played out in historical time. The atonement that accomplished our redemption was a real-time, definitive, historical atonement.

Let us look closely again at Jesus Christ of Nazareth as he makes his messianic claim. Here is one who clearly partakes of our full, though sinless, humanity. We say that here is the Son of God, and we say, too, that here is the man Christ Jesus. What are we to say of the Person of Jesus Christ? Was he, then, a human person? To say that he was, would be to say that not only did he come from the eternity in which he had existed with the Father and the Spirit, but that by a transformation about which the Scriptures do not speak he ceased to be God. Such a claim, moreover, would belie the necessity of his coming and the respect in which that necessity determined the possibility of our redemption. For it was impossible that a human person could have wrought our redemption. What we have already seen about the realities of the Fall and of sin stand in the way of any possibility of our redemption by a human person.

Are we to say, then, that Jesus Christ of Nazareth was, in some sense that we should then endeavor to unravel, a divine-human person? Presumably, the meaning of such a claim would be that he was a person in whom the divine and the human natures were commingled or blended together in a manner that, by virtue of their interfusion and interpenetration, rendered it impossible to say that the one confronting us was either uniquely divine or uniquely human. Again our answer must be in the negative. Jesus Christ was not a human person. He was not a divine-human person. We are required to say that Jesus Christ was a divine Person. He was a unique Person. No person like him had appeared on the scene of human history before.

The eternal Son of God did, in fact, in coming into the world, take to himself a truly human nature, being born of the virgin and thereby truly man. He came in a human body that had been prepared for him by the Holy Spirit in the womb of the virgin Mary. He assumed to himself a true and reasonable human soul, with all of the faculties of soul that we have discussed in previous contexts. He took into union with his divine nature a truly human nature, yet without sin. But in combining the two natures in his one Person, that Person was, and continues to be, a divine Person. In him, the human nature was not personalized.

He has been called the theanthropic Person, combining the Greek words "theos" meaning God and "anthropos" meaning man. He was the God-man. The designation is appropriate, provided it is understood to imply the careful distinctions that orthodox theology has found it necessary to make.

Doctrinal controversies and their settlement

To understand the answers that must be given to the questions we have raised it will be useful to look at some earlier controversies related to the Person of Christ. The biblical doctrine of the person of Christ quickly came under attack, even in the apostolic times. In his letter to the Colossian church Paul was concerned to refute certain heresies that were akin to what later became a more fully developed Gnosticism, and John in his epistle was very much concerned with the same problem. Gnosticism in its many expressions and aspects was essentially a heresy that denied the reality of the deity and the divinity of Christ. It argued, for example, that there could not have been a true union of spirit with matter. Divinity, in which essential goodness inhered, could not come into union with humanity and matter and material substance in which, as it was supposed, evil inhered. It was impossible, therefore, it was claimed, that Jesus Christ could be both divine and human. One expression of Gnosticism argued that Jesus Christ was a man on whom and to whom the Spirit of God came at an early stage of his life and ministry, but that the Spirit departed from him before his death. A heresy akin to Gnosticism was that known as Docetism, which denied that Christ was in fact a man by claiming that he possessed only a phantom body.

We do not pause at this time to consider all of the erroneous doctrines related to the Person of our Lord. But a brief note of one interesting development that came into prominence following the Reformation will add precision in our own doctrinal statement. The Lutheran theology, for example, departed from the doctrine of the other Reformers and constructed a unique doctrine of the Person of Christ. What that system amounts to is the claim that at the incarnation the attributes of each of the natures of Christ, the divine and the human, were communicated to the other nature. The Reformed churches held, to the contrary, that the attributes of each nature are communicated only to the one Person, and that that one Person existed in both natures. The Lutheran doctrine therefore held that "at the moment of the incarnation, in virtue of the union between the divine and the human natures, the human nature of Christ became omniscient, omnipotent, and omnipresent."[4]

---

[4] A. A. Hodge, *Evangelical Theology*, 195.

A fuller discussion of the Lutheran scheme of doctrine, moreover, reveals a further, but erroneous, implication of it. That has to do with the doctrine of the sacrament of the Lord's Supper. Luther did replace the Roman Catholic doctrine of *transubstantiation*, whereby the bread and the wine were imagined actually to be changed into the real body and blood of Christ, with his doctrine that became known as *consubstantiation*. That claimed, not that the elements of the Supper were changed in the manner that the Roman Catholic doctrine had supposed, but that in the Supper the body and blood of Christ was present "*in, with, and under*" the bread and wine. But if, as is said by that claim, the human nature of Christ became omnipresent, along with the divine nature, and if, as a result, his body and blood are omnipresent, then they must be present not only in the bread and wine of the sacrament, but "*in, with, and under*" all food and drink. But the Scriptures do not support such a claim of the commingling of the eternal and the temporal. In making those observations, however, we have gone ahead of our subject. We stay for the moment with the problems that arose by virtue of other heretical claims that pressed on the early church. In the post-apostolic age problems similar to those we have mentioned arose. The Sabellians argued that the Son and the Father were not distinct persons but only different aspects or emanations of the one Being. Arius, an Alexandrian priest, claimed that the Son was not equal with the Father, but that he was created by him. Orthodoxy was thus forced to articulate the doctrine of the person of Christ in such a way as to avoid the Sabellian heresy on the one side and that of the Arians on the other.[5]

The Arian heresy was condemned by the church at the Council of Nicea in the year 325.[6] An important figure in the early history of the church, Athanasius, who became Bishop

---

[5] For further discussion see Vickers, *Divine Redemption*.
[6] See Philip Schaff, *The Creeds of Christendom* (Grand Rapids: Baker, 1983), vol. 1, 24.

of Alexandria in 328, argued strongly for the Nicean orthodoxy. The church steadily adhered to that position. The continuing problems surrounding the church's Christology, or its doctrine of the person of Christ, were confronted and settled definitively at the Council of Chalcedon in 451 A.D. That Council has become justly famous for its achievement of what has become referred to as the Christological settlement.[7]

The Creed of Chalcedon gave expression to the doctrine of the Person of Christ by stating that the divine and the human natures were so related in him as to be "two natures, without confusion, without change, without division, without separation." In the first two of those statements, without confusion and without change, a safeguard is erected against the idea that the two natures are in any sense intermingled. The last two explanatory statements assert the full reality of the union of the natures.

The implications of the incarnation in real historical time

The reality of the incarnation, notwithstanding the mystery of it, and the reality, at the same time, of the divine personhood of our Lord, raise again the significance of two points that we have already mentioned. We have spoken of the holiness of God and, as intrinsic to his holiness, his separateness from all of created reality external to himself. That implies his eternal separateness from time. That separateness comes to significant focus in relation to the knowledge that God possesses, not only of himself, but of all of the eventuation of all of the histories of created entities. It thereby takes up the fact of God's foreknowledge and foreordination of all that eventuates, and thereby the certainty and the security of the redemption that God has set forth.

We have spoken also of the attributes and the knowledge of God. It follows from what we have just said, then, that the

[7] Ibid., 29.

person of Jesus Christ, as he walked in this world as the eternal Son of God, remaining as he did very God of very God, continued in full possession of those same attributes, holiness, and knowledge. In short, in his coming into the world he did not lay aside his divine identity and glory. He did, as the scriptural data make clear, lay aside in many respects the insignia or the demonstrable signs of his glory. But he was, and he continued to be, one with the Father. Staggering as the realization is, we may observe something of the significance of it.

It has been a common misunderstanding of the Person of our Lord in this respect to claim that when he came into the world he did, in some sense, lay aside his divine attributes. Such a teaching might appear to be supported by the paragraph in the second chapter of Paul's letter to the Philippians on which it is supposedly based. Our Lord, as Paul says there, "made himself of no reputation, and took upon him the form of a servant, and was made in the likeness of men; and being found in fashion as a man, he humbled himself ..." (Phil. 2:7-8). Where both the King James Version and the New King James Version state that Christ "made himself of no reputation," the Greek text has the word *ekenosen* which means, literally, "emptied" himself. It is from that Greek word that the teaching we have referred to, known as the "kenotic" theory, derives its claim. But the Philippian passage does not bear such an interpretation. As the KJV and the NKJV translations have it, it is plainly concerned with the manner in which the Second Person of the Godhead humbled himself in order that he might be our redeemer.

It is true that many aspects of the life and experiences and actions of our Lord that are uniquely attributable to his human nature are, in fact, attributed in the Scripture to his person. Similarly, many actions and expressions and realizations that are as clearly and uniquely referable to his divine nature are also attributed to his person. But we should understand in considering those facts that his Person, in all its uniqueness and individual identity, was determined essentially by his divine nature. By this we mean that the divine nature dominated and determined and controlled the human nature and its actions and activities.

That is clear from a brief consideration of only one point of fact in relation to him. We know that he was sinless. We know that as to his human nature he grew, that he was ignorant of certain things, and learned, and developed to maturity. How, then, could it have been true that in his human ignorance he remained free from sin? Are we to say that he was not humanly ignorant of anything? If we were to do so, we should contradict the Scriptures. And yet we say that he did not sin. Do we say, then, that he was impeccable, meaning that it was impossible for him to sin? On the basis of scriptural testimony as to his person we have to say that he was. It was impossible for him to sin. We must work out our doctrine carefully to that effect.

The impeccability of Christ

The claim of impeccability, it is important to keep in mind, is a claim that is made of the *Person* of Jesus Christ. He was an impeccable person whose human nature was tempted and was itself capable of sin. But in Christ the human nature was in no sense the isolated human nature in which we, as Adam's posterity, exist. In Christ, the human nature was joined in union with a divine nature. And the divine nature so dominated and determined the scope of action and supervised the human nature that it was impossible that *in his Person* Christ could sin. What the human nature might have been capable of, in and of itself, it was incapable of when it was joined with the divine nature in the divine Person of Christ. We observed in an earlier context that while our Lord took unto himself a human nature, that nature was not in him personalized. In his very valuable discussion of "the unipersonality of Christ," Berkhof has made the same point, where he observes that "the

Logos assumed a human nature that was not personalized, that did not exist by itself."[8]

That important doctrine of the relation between the divine and the human natures of Christ can be considered further. We have said in effect that the divine nature did not permit the human nature to sin, not even as Jesus of Nazareth in whom the natures were combined grew and learned until his maturity. But there came a point in time, of course, at which the divine nature permitted the human nature to suffer in a unique and eternally significant sense. In his human nature Christ suffered for us when he bore the penalty for our sins on the cross. At that point he knew, in his cry of dereliction, that he was bearing the wrath of the Father, that he was thereby satisfying divine justice on behalf of the sinners for whom he died. It was only in that way that their redemption could be achieved.

The Scriptures that bear on the Person of Christ, we saw in our discussion of the doctrine of God, imply that the divine mind was wholly in the Father and the Spirit and wholly in the Son. And we have seen that it was the eternal divine identity of the Son that was incarnate in Jesus Christ. He came into this world from his pre-existence with the Father. It follows that Christ in his divine nature continued, in all his Godhood, his divine existence outside of time. When he walked in this world Christ was, as to his divine nature, in this world and also continually present with the Father in heaven. As to his human nature, he was present on earth. That is the great mystery of the incarnation. We bow before it and acknowledge that its truth establishes the reality of our redemption and our reconciliation with God.

---

[8] Berkhof, *Systematic Theology*, 321-22. See also W.G.T. Shedd, *Dogmatic Theology* (Grand Rapids: Zondervan, Reprint, n.d.), vol. 2, 330.

The atonement and the high priesthood of Christ in human nature in time

Our doctrine states that at the incarnation Christ, the Son of God, took into union with his divine nature a true human nature, meaning by that a true body and a reasonable soul. He knew and thought and willed and suffered as a man. It was in his human nature that, as the writer to the Hebrews states, he "learned obedience by the things which he suffered" in order that, "being made perfect, he became the author of eternal salvation unto all them that obey him" (Heb. 5:8-9). It was necessary that in order to qualify to serve as our high priest Christ should be made "perfect through sufferings" (Heb. 2:10). That being so, "in that he himself hath suffered being tempted, he is able to succour them that are tempted" (Heb. 2:18). We therefore "have a great high priest ... not an high priest which cannot be touched with the feeling of our infirmities; but [one who] was in all points tempted like as we are, yet without sin." Therefore, we may "come boldly unto the throne of grace, that we may obtain mercy, and find grace to help in time of need" (Heb. 4:14-16).

The letter to the Hebrews is saying that the focus of our thought must fall on the fact that it is Christ *incarnate* who is thus presented to us as our high priest. It is the incarnate Christ who lived and died for us, and who, by his active and his passive obedience, purchased a title to heaven for us. It was in his human nature that our redeemer died and rose again. It is in his human nature that he ascended and sits "at the right hand of the Majesty on high" (Heb. 1:3). It is in his human nature that he makes intercession for us, and it is in his human nature that he is coming again to receive us to himself.

While all of that is a necessary part of our doctrine of the Person of our Lord, an important statement remains to be made regarding his work of atonement in his messianic-mediatorial assignment. We shall return in more detail to Christ's work of atonement in the next chapter. But an important point to be made at present follows from the fact that, as we emphasized at the beginning, in the incarnation the Second Person of the Godhead entered into the process of time that he himself had created. That, we have said, is the ultimate mystery of the incarnation.

But in the incarnation of Christ there did not occur, and there could not have occurred, any commingling or mixing of the eternal and the temporal. By that we mean that the eternal, or all that characterized our Lord as the eternal Son of God, did not cease to be relevant and important in its own right. And similarly, the temporal, or what it was of existence in time that characterized the incarnate Son of God, continued and remained relevant in its own right. In other words, in the person of Christ there was no commingling or intermingling of the divine and the human natures. On this ground we can observe that in God's design and implementation of the plan of our redemption there was similarly, at all points and in every respect, no commingling of the eternal and the temporal. We must work that out a little more fully.

The eternal and the temporal, we have said, remained separate and unimpaired in their respective relevances. That is, the eternal remained timeless, and the eternal character of Christ remained unchanged, with all of the attributes of the Godhead essential to it. And the temporal, or the human nature of Christ, that was itself created by the divine agency of the Holy Spirit, retained its temporal and its finite character. Because that was so, we must say that as the objectives in view in the accomplishment of redemption were realized, the eternal and the temporal were not commingled at any stage. They were not commingled in the incarnation of the Son of God. But it follows that they could not be commingled at the atonement he made. It was, as we have said, in his human nature that he assumed in time that Christ bore our sin.

But a further implication is to be noted. It follows with equal necessity that neither could the eternal and the temporal be commingled at the point of the sinner's salvation, or at his transition from wrath to grace. No commingling could occur at the point at which the sinner is translated by the work of God from the kingdom of darkness into the kingdom of his dear Son (Col. 1:13). That is so because, first, our salvation, the Scriptures make clear, is all of grace. It is by the grace of God that we are saved (Eph. 2:8). It is by the grace of God set forth in the divine Person of his Son that salvation in all its parts is provided for us. It is God himself, in that gracious provision, who makes his Son to be unto us "wisdom and righteousness and sanctification and redemption" (1 Cor. 1:30). Only by the sovereign grace of God, reaching from eternity beyond the createdness of time in which we are bound, are we rescued from the ignorance, guilt, pollution, and misery into which we had fallen by reason of Adam's sin.

But second, when we say there is no commingling of the eternal and the temporal in the sinner's transition from wrath to grace, and when we say that our salvation is entirely due to the operation of the grace of God, we mean that the creation of the new life in the soul, the work of regeneration by which the sinner receives the gift of faith that turns him to Christ, is completely and solely the sovereign, unsolicited work of the Holy Spirit of God. That important conclusion can be stated in a different way. The very faith by which the sinner believes in Christ is itself the gift of God. The sinner, that is, is passive in his regeneration and has no part in it and can take no merit from it.

The necessary point may be made still differently. Regeneration, we say, is prior to faith. It is not the case that a person is born again because he has faith in Christ. If that were true, then salvation would depend, at the crucial point of regeneration, on a joint work of both God and man. And contrary to our doctrine, that would imply that the eternal (the grace of God) and the temporal (the activity of the sinner) would have been, to use our expression, commingled. There would then be a joint activity of the grace of God on the one hand and human effort and merit on the other. That is what would be meant by the commingling of the eternal and the temporal at the point of the sinner's regeneration. That, however, we reject. The reality is that a person believes in Christ because he has been born again. And that new birth is effected in the soul by the sovereign work of the eternal Spirit of God. The correct understanding of our doctrine on that important point clarifies the difference between the Arminian and the Reformed doctrines of salvation. We shall return to that important point of doctrine.

Final implications of the doctrine of the Person of Christ

In the light of what we have said, a final point can be made. First, in the incarnate Son of God eternity and time have been brought into a new relation, one that will itself continue throughout the eternal age that is still ahead. Having assumed our human nature to himself, our Lord has not divested himself of it. Nor will he do so. "In like manner as ye have seen him go into heaven," the angels declared, "this same Jesus shall come" (Acts 1:11). "It doth not yet appear what we shall be; but when he shall appear we shall be like him" (1 John 3:2). In the very nature of the case, it is not possible that we shall transcend our finitude or our humanness. But in our humanity we shall see our Savior in the humanity that he assumed to himself, and we shall be like him.

Finally, when we say that in Christ the eternal and the temporal have been brought into a new relation, we recognize that it was in actual and real historical time that that occurred and our redemption was accomplished. The glory of the gospel is that the atonement was a real-time, historic atonement. Christ, in the human nature that he assumed in historical time, died for our sins in historical time. Now in his mysterious supervision of the becoming as well as the being of his redeemed people, God by his works of providence and the ministry of his Spirit is immanent in historical time to bring us to glory.

Nothing, surely, is more designed to evoke the wonder and the worship of the people of God than the realities we have just considered. That worship and praise spill over, in the life and walk of the believer, in a determination to lay aside all else and follow in the way of righteousness that God in Christ has marked out for us. Where else is the motivation to love the law of God grounded than in the realization of the fullness of grace that he has set forth in his Son for our benefit? For we whom he has redeemed are the beneficiaries of all the benefits and blessings that were stated in the terms of the covenant of grace.

We shall look in more detail in the following chapter at our Lord's execution of his high priestly office and his redemptive accomplishment for us. And we shall see that by virtue of the Holy Spirit's work, all of the benefits of Christ's redemptive atonement are communicated to us. We shall see that it is the committed task and office of the Holy Spirit to conduct to glory those whom Christ redeemed.

Chapter 7

The Redemptive Office of Christ

The cross of Christ stands as the watershed of human history. The covenant of grace worked out its unswerving course from Eden to Golgotha, and the Prince of peace paid in his human death the penalty for the sins of his people. The cross has ever been "to them that perish foolishness" (1 Cor. 1:18). But its stark report, its message that neither angels nor men in all eternity can plumb, speaks rescue and relief to sinners tortured in the state to which Adam's Fall reduced them. Here is mystery of mysteries, that God in flesh dies to provide a redemption for sinners. The reality and the necessity of the case were such that only incarnate Deity could pay the price that the honor and justice of Deity demanded.

The cross of Christ culminates the covenantal promise. A number of questions and issues arise as we contemplate the redemptive office of Christ. We are chastened and cautioned to let our thought be bound to the Word of God as we see him completing his messianic-mediatorial assignment. Beyond the covenantal context of redemption, the necessity and the extent of the atonement, the obedience of Christ, his High Priesthood, and his heavenly priestly office call for reflection and comment.

We have anticipated much that we must consider under the present heading. We saw at an early stage that the terms and the process of our redemption are what they are because they were ordained in the predeterminate council of the Godhead before the foundation of the world. They are expressed doctrinally in what we have referred to as the *Covenant of Redemption* between the Persons of the Godhead which established the redemptive offices of the Father, the Son, and the Holy Spirit. The objectives of that covenant of redemption have been progressively realized by God's providential working in the world. He has done that through successive forms of administration of the *Covenant of Grace*. That covenant he established with his people as represented by Christ. Those successive forms of administration have been observed in human history in the initial covenant with Abraham, in the highly institutionalized Mosaic administration whose ceremonies anticipated and pointed to the coming of Christ, and then in the "new covenant" that God promised through the prophet Jeremiah. That promise was fulfilled in the incarnation and the redemptive work of the very Son of God (Jer. 31:31, 33; Heb. 10:16).

The redemptive work that Christ completed in this world has frequently been studied under the heading of "the satisfaction of Christ." That historic designation is highly appropriate. By it we refer to the satisfaction which, in his life and by his substitutionary death, Christ provided to the justice and the law of God and to God's wrath against the sinner and his sin. We must now work out the manner in which that satisfaction emanates from our Lord's voluntary undertaking of his messianic-redemptive assignment. He discharged that assignment by his obedience in this world to the demands of it, and by his continuing discharge on our behalf of his heavenly high priesthood.

We may speak by way of summary of the "redemptive

complex of the Christ-event." That "redemptive complex" takes up a series of real historical events and occurrences that together encompass the work of Christ. We refer in that to (i) the incarnation, (ii) the obedience, (iii) the death, (iv) the resurrection, (v) the ascension, (vi) the heavenly session and high priesthood, and (vii) the coming again of our Lord. We begin by recalling the covenantal context of the redemption that Christ accomplished.

The covenantal context of redemption

We note at this point a minimal amount of scriptural witness to the covenantal significance of the coming and the work of Christ. We have it in that most familiar of all texts that "God so loved the world that he *gave* his only begotten son" (John 3:16). The Son of God came to die for his people because God gave his Son for that purpose. John again says in his first epistle that God "*sent* his Son to be the propitiation for our sins" (1 John 4:10). The Son came into the world, he was sent into the world, because from before the foundation of the world it was ordained that our redemption could be accomplished only by that means.

Paul clarifies the fact that "God the Father ... hath chosen us in him before the foundation of the world ... having predestinated us unto the adoption of children by Jesus Christ to himself, according to the good pleasure of his will" (Eph. 1:4-5). Peter also sets the argument of his epistle against the design of the same predeterminate council. He is writing, he says, to the "elect according to the foreknowledge of God the Father, through sanctification of the Spirit, unto obedience and sprinkling of the blood of Christ" (1 Peter 1:2). Peter displays there the separate and distinctive offices of the three persons of the Godhead who are actively engaged in effecting our redemption.

The Old Testament Scriptures are replete with the statement of God's covenantal purpose and with the history of his providential movement to its consummation. Those Scriptures insist repeatedly on God's jealousy for his covenant and his faithfulness to the terms of it. In that context, Malachi, the last of the Old Testament prophets, addresses the priests and conveys God's complaint against them for the way they had failed in their covenantal responsibilities. He spoke at length against the ways in which the priests at that time had turned their backs on their obligations under the covenant of priesthood. That covenant of priesthood was, of course, a crucial aspect of the earlier form of administration of the covenant of grace. The priests, Malachi charged, had "corrupted the covenant of Levi" and they had "profaned the covenant of our fathers" (Mal. 2:8,10). That, as a careful reading of the Old Testament reveals, was God's repeated complaint against his people. In various ways and in varying situations they had denied the obligations of the covenant in terms of which God had called them to be his people. Nothing brings to more sensitive or articulate focus God's charge of infidelity against his people, or their adultery from him as it is repeatedly referred to, than the complaint that they had denied and rejected the covenantal obligations for which they were liable.

But in his prophecy Malachi exults in the promise that "the Lord ... the messenger of the covenant ... shall come" (Mal. 3:1); and again, "the Sun of righteousness shall arise with healing in his wings" (Mal. 4:2). God will be faithful to his eternal commitment. He will infallibly redeem his people. His anointed One, the promised Messiah, the "messenger of the covenant," the "Sun of righteousness," will fully discharge his redemptive office and he will "save his people" (Matt. 1:21). It is God's faithfulness to the covenant he established that conducts us to the meaning of the work of Christ for us. He came in order that, as the prophet Daniel had promised, "in the midst of the week" he might "confirm the covenant with many" (Dan. 9:27). In that climactic moment to which all of history pointed he brought in the new kingdom of righteousness.

We could extend the scriptural testimony. But that is hardly necessary at this time. The prophets, who spoke repeatedly of Christ (John 5:39), spread their testimony lavishly across the pages of the sacred text. "Surely he hath borne our griefs and carried our sorrows.... He was wounded for our transgressions, he was bruised for our iniquities, the chastisement of our peace was upon him, and with his stripes we are healed.... The Lord hath laid upon him the iniquity of us all.... It pleased the Lord to bruise him [and] to make his soul an offering for sin.... He hath poured out his soul unto death, and he was numbered with the transgressors, and he bare the sin of many" (Is. 53:4-6, 10-12). Here we come face to face with the heart of the gospel. God, who is eternally faithful to the oath that he swore and to his promise of redemption, has himself borne in Christ the penalties, the curse of malediction, that justly accrued to us.

The necessity of the atonement

In the light of what has been said of the covenantal structure of redemption, we focus our discussion on two questions. First, why do we say that the atonement of Christ was necessary? And second, for whom, when he came, did Christ die, and who, therefore, are the beneficiaries of the redemption he provided? Erroneous answers to both these questions, it must sadly be acknowledged, have betrayed the testimony of the church at various times in the course of its history.

When we consider the *necessity* of the atonement of Christ we are not now speaking, as we have done at length already, of the fact that it was necessary that the penalty for our sin should be paid. We ask, first, at a more fundamental level, whether it was necessary that God should set forth a plan of redemption. When we considered earlier God's electing decree we saw that the subjects of that decree were fallen people, a defined and certain number from among Adam and his fallen posterity. But now we are asking whether it was *necessary* that God should redeem. And our answer to that question must clearly be "no." It was in no sense necessary that God should redeem. His righteousness and justice would have remained inviolate if he had left all of mankind to the eternal damnation that their choice in Adam warranted. But the reality is that according to his sovereign will, and by his mercy and for his own glory, he elected to save some.

But then, God having chosen to redeem, the question arose as to how that redemption was to be accomplished. If we may speak with caution in such terms, that was the problem that eternally confronted the heavens. In responding to that question, doctrinal error has arisen regarding the necessity of the atonement of Christ. There are those who say that when God had chosen to redeem, then because he was the sovereign God he was perfectly free to redeem by any method he chose. If he had chosen to do so, it is said, he could have redeemed simply by declaring certain people righteous. To claim anything to the contrary would violate irremediably the sovereignty of God who is free to do as he wills in heaven and earth. In actual fact he did, as we know, choose to effect redemption by means of the substitutionary death of his Son. But, the teaching we have referred to says, it was not *absolutely necessary* that salvation should have been by that means. The atonement that Christ did in fact effect, so the argument goes, was not an *absolute necessity*, but was only what we should have to refer to as a *hypothetical necessity*.

What, then, is to be said? Was the atonement of Christ an *absolute necessity*, or only a *hypothetical necessity*? The answer we give takes us to the heart of the gospel. We concur with John Murray, a prominent twentieth-century theologian, in his conclusion that the atonement was a *consequent absolute necessity*.[1] The meaning of that statement is that while redemption itself was not necessary, nevertheless when God

---

[1] John Murray, *Redemption – Accomplished and Applied* (Grand Rapids: Eerdmans, 1955), 13-22.

did choose to redeem there was only one way in which redemption could be effected. Consequent on God's decision to redeem, it was an absolute necessity that redemption should be accomplished by his sending his eternal, self-existent Son into the world for that purpose. The Son would take a sinless human nature into union with his divine nature and in that human nature bear the penalty for our sin.

The extent of the atonement

When we refer to the extent of the atonement we are asking quite simply, who was it for whom Christ died? The answer, which has not, unfortunately, gained the universal agreement of the church in the course of its history, is that Christ died for those whom the Father gave him to redeem. We have noted our Lord's acknowledgment of that fact when he prayed in his High Priestly prayer, "Thine they were, and thou gavest them me" (John 17:6). But it is necessary at this point to see the question in the light of the covenantal objectives and processes that God has established.

Recalling our discussion of the divine covenants, we approach our present question by asking, first, who were the subjects of the covenant of redemption? By that we mean who, in the mind and the electing wisdom of God, were contemplated as the beneficiaries of the redemption that the triune Persons of the Godhead designed? Our answer has been that they were the definite, numbered, and unalterable set of people, from among Adam and his posterity who had fallen into the state of sin, upon whom God set his electing love. We saw that the wonder of that situation and condition was not that God failed to elect everybody to eternal life, but that when all deserved nothing but the eternal perdition their sin warranted God had mercy on some. We saw that difficulties in concurring with the fact and the biblical doctrine of God's predestinating covenant emanate from a failure to grasp the radical nature of the biblical explanation of sin and the Fall.

Without recapitulating what has been said as to its terms, we ask the same question of the covenant of grace that God set forth, his covenantal commitment to those whom he had chosen to redeem in Christ. Who, we ask again, were the subjects of that covenant and decree? The answer must be that they were the same people, in their individuality and particularity, who were the subjects of the covenant of redemption. They were the people for whom Christ died. There was not, and there could not be, any disparity between the work of God the Father in his election and the work of God the Son in his dying for his people. The subjects of the decree to elect and the decree to redeem were necessarily the same set of people.

The implications of the biblical doctrine can be extended. We have observed the redemptive offices of the Persons of the Godhead and their distinctive operations. The redemptive office of the Father was to elect. That of the Son was to redeem. That of the Holy Spirit is to call and sanctify and conduct to glory those whom the Father chose and whom the Son redeemed. We contemplate in that statement a common set of people who were the subjects of each of the covenantal decrees, undertakings, and objectives. That important biblical doctrine can be seen in clear light by supposing, for a moment, that the contrary of it is true.

It was observed a moment ago that a wedge would be driven between the works of the Father and the Son if the subjects of the Father's election were in any sense different from the subjects of the Son's redemption. Similarly now, if it were imagined that the subjects of the Holy Spirit's effectual call and sanctifying work were different from the subjects of the Son's redemption, a wedge would be driven between the work of the Son and the work of the Holy Spirit. But from any such imagination a fatal denial of biblical doctrine follows. For if, in the ways we have suggested, a wedge is driven between the *works* of the Persons of the Godhead, that implies that a wedge is driven between the *knowledge* of those Persons. But then, with all too clear fatality, that implies that a wedge is driven between the *being* of the Persons of the Godhead. And that means that the biblical doctrine of the unity and simplicity of the Godhead is destroyed. Such, it should now be seen, are the terrible results and implications of the refusal to hold to the biblical doctrine of the particularity of the atonement that Christ provided. We are forced to hold to the particularity of all of God's covenantal designs.

The evangelical church at large, however, has not held uniformly to the biblical gospel at these important points. The question that has troubled the church throughout its history is whether Christ did not die, as the expression goes, for all men indiscriminately? We hold, consistently with what has now been said, that Christ died for a particular people. We hold a doctrine of *particular atonement.* If, on the contrary, we were to say that Christ died for all men indiscriminately we would hold a doctrine of general or *universal atonement.*

It is claimed by those who insist on a universal atonement that to hold anything different commits the error of limiting the atonement. But that charge can be readily shown to be in error. For consider what is involved in it. Those who say that Christ died for all men indiscriminately are necessarily saying that in his death Christ paid the penalty of the sins of all men. But if that is so, then why, it must be asked, are not all men saved? For it is clear on adequate biblical grounds, terrible in its contemplation though the reality is, that some are left to eternal perdition. And not being saved, why is it the case then that in spite of Christ's having borne the penalty for their guilt they are still left to bear it again for themselves in eternity?

The answer that is given by the universal atonement theory is that such people are not saved because they do not accept the salvation that Christ has provided for them. They are left to eternal perdition because of their sin of unbelief. But that implies that Christ bore the penalty of their sin in vain, or to no effective purpose or result. For if the sin of unbelief continues, as has just been said, there remains that one sin for which Christ did not bear the penalty. There exists, therefore, a flat contradiction of the claim at the beginning of the "universal atonement" argument that Christ bore every person's sin. Or perhaps a line of escape from the contradictory conclusion may exist in the supposition that Christ bore, not all, but only some of the sins of all people. But that escape route leads to a dead end also. For what it does is to clarion loudly that the atonement is, after all, a limited atonement. The contradiction remains. Either the atonement that Christ provided in accordance with the will and the covenantal design of the Godhead is a limited atonement as to its extent, or it is limited as to its efficacy. The theory of universal atonement holds to the latter, and in doing so it must be seen as an unacceptable rejection of the biblical doctrine. To establish that, it is necessary only to recall that our Lord himself made it clear that he came to give his life for his "sheep" (John 10:15). He "loved the church and gave himself for it" (Eph. 5:25). He came, as Matthew says in his gospel, "to save *his people* from their sins" (Matt. 1:21). We hold not only to the fact of a particular atonement, but to the fact that in his death Christ actually saved his people. He did not die only to make their salvation possible. We reject every suggestion of a possibility theory of salvation, such as is inherent in the claim that Christ provided, in some sense, a universal atonement.

That erroneous view of the atonement that Christ provided follows in the footsteps of an old but tenacious and dangerous error. It is not with any pleasure or satisfaction that we are forced to say that Pelagius in the fourth century, the Arminians in the seventeenth century, Wesley in the eighteenth century, and the Billy Graham evangelistic enterprise in the last century, hold, in these respects, a seriously sub-biblical doctrine. The defect involves a shallow and misleading doctrine of the state of man as he exists as a result of Adam's Fall. The claim of universal atonement carries with it the erroneous doctrine that in the state in which he now exists man has within him by his own volition the ability and power to turn to God and accept the salvation which, it is supposed, Christ has purchased for him. But that is far from the scriptural truth. We saw in a previous chapter that the condition of the faculties of the soul in the state of sin is such that man is not free to turn to God. He is the blinded slave of the Devil. The universal atonement theory holds a defective doctrine of the meaning and the result of the Fall that dragged us all down into sin. It is not necessary to repeat at this point what was said on that level when we discussed the doctrine of sin.

The universal atonement theology implies that man is perfectly free to accept or reject the offered salvation that Christ provided. That means, essentially, that in the last analysis man saves himself. For he retains to himself the sovereign decision as to whether he will accept or reject Christ. But if man is sovereign in any part of his salvation, God in Christ has thereby been robbed of the sovereignty that is his. We concur with the scriptural declaration that God is sovereign in all parts of our salvation. He is sovereign in electing us to salvation, in providing redemption for us in Christ, in renewing us in mind, heart, and will by his Holy Spirit's work of regeneration within us, and in conducting us to glory.

The obedience of Christ

What was the means by which Christ accomplished the redemption he came to provide for us? The answer must turn on what it was that the law of God required to be done. It then follows that Christ has saved us from the wrath of God, or that, to state it in different terms, he has given us a title to heaven. He did that by reason of his obedience to what was required of him and what he had undertaken to do before the foundation of the world. In short, it is the obedience of Christ that saves us. Paul stated that with precise clarity in his letter to the Romans. "As by one man's [Adam's] disobedience many were made sinners, so by the obedience of one [Christ] shall many be made righteous" (Rom. 5:19). What, then, is involved in the obedience of Christ?

We must look, first, at the requirements of God's holy law. Adam, in his Fall that dragged us all down into sin, repudiated the holy demands of that law. The law was broken and its mandates remained unfulfilled. The situation that therefore existed was twofold. First, as the law had been broken, and as it had been broken in human nature, the penalty for breaking the law must be paid, and it must be paid in human nature. But secondly, in order that God's honor and justice should not be violated, the law must be kept. A twofold requirement thus came into effect. The penalty for breaking the law must be paid, and the law itself must be kept.

When Christ came as our substitute in human nature it was necessary that he should do two things. First, it was necessary for him to render a perfect obedience to the law, so that it could then be said that he was our substitute in keeping the law. And second, he was required to pay the penalty that was due to us for our having broken the law. That double requirement Christ precisely fulfilled for us. His perfect keeping of the law is referred to doctrinally as his *active obedience*. And the fact that he died in our place is referred to doctrinally as his *passive obedience*. When we say that it is the *obedience* of Christ that gives us our title to heaven, we include in that our recognition of both his active and his passive obedience. The significance of that can be seen in a slightly different way.

If all that Christ did for us was to bear the penalty of our sin by dying as our substitute, the guilt of our having broken God's law might be regarded as having been dealt with. But while that was so, it would still remain that the law would, in the future, have to be kept. And if Christ had not kept it for us, then we would be left to keep it for ourselves. But that, it follows from all we have said, was the very thing we could not do. Our case, then, would be no better than before. We should still be left undone in the presence of God and his holy law. But what, we can ask again, did Christ do for us? The answer is that he did all that was necessary, and in doing it, he did for us what we could not do for ourselves. He was our substitute in keeping the law, and he was our substitute in bearing the penalty for our having broken the law. That, in its comprehensive compass, is the measure of what the obedience of Christ means for us.

In all of the work of Christ as our substitute there was a deliberateness, a steadfastness by which he discharged impeccably the obligations that he had assumed as our Redeemer. His dedication to those obligations was noted at a highly climactic point in his earthly career. At the conclusion of his Galileean ministry Christ "steadfastly set his face to go to Jerusalem" (Luke 9:51). He must needs go to Jerusalem. He must needs pursue to the end the objectives for which he had come into the world. He must give his life for his people. At that climactic moment he deliberately chose the way of the cross. The work of Christ in this world, the atonement he provided, together with his impeccable keeping the law, was an actual historical obedience in actual historical time. The death that he suffered in his human nature was an actual death in which he sustained "the sorrows of death" and "the pains of hell" (Ps. 116:3) on the sinner's behalf. It was after his cry of dereliction on the cross that he could say, "It is finished," and our redemption was accomplished. As our high priest, the antitype of the priestly administrations in the earlier and anticipatory dispensation, he "once offered up himself" (Heb. 7:27), and "by his own blood he entered in once into the holy place, having obtained eternal redemption for us" (Heb. 9:12). Unlike the repetitive offerings of the anticipatory priestly administrations, Christ "now once in the end of the world appeared to put away sin by the sacrifice of himself." He was "once offered to bear the sins of many" (Heb. 9:26, 28). Again, Peter has observed: "Christ also hath once suffered for sins, the just for the unjust, that he might bring us to God" (1 Peter 3:18). Peter has summarized the gospel at this point. We are redeemed, he says, not with "corruptible things ... but with the precious blood of Christ ... who verily was foreordained before the foundation of the world" (1 Peter 1:18-20); and Christ "his own self bore our sins in his own body on the tree, that we, being dead to sins, should live unto righteousness, by whose stripes ye were healed" (1 Peter 2:24). Christ was the priest who made the offering for sin, and he was himself the offering. He offered himself to God for us. He was in every sense "the Lamb of God, which taketh away the sin of the world" (John 1:29).

The high priestly office of Christ

We referred at the beginning of this chapter to the "redemptive complex of the Christ-event." A further aspect of that complex of events has to do with Christ's office as our high priest. He has discharged an earthly high priestly office for us and now, in his session at the right hand of the Father, he discharges his heavenly high priestly office on our behalf.

Christ, we saw in an earlier context, was not a human person. He was, and he remains, a divine Person who took into union with his divine nature a perfect and sinless human nature. At the completion of his messianic-mediatorial assignment he did not, he could not, and he never will, divest himself of that human nature. That means that following his resurrection and his ascension he lives now in heaven in the human nature that he assumed for our redemption. There is One in heaven, that is, who was in fact, as the writer to the Hebrews has said, "touched with the feelings of our infirmities," who was "in all points tempted as we are, yet without sin," and "in that he himself hath suffered being tempted [is] able to succour them that are tempted" (Heb. 4:15; 2:18). The angels said to the disciples who watched as our Lord was taken from them into heaven, "This same Jesus [we note that at that point his human name is used] which is taken up from you into heaven, shall so come in like manner as ye have seen him go into heaven" (Acts 1:11). As our Lord died, arose, and ascended in his human nature, so he will return in his human nature to take us to himself for ever.

That brings to emphasis the fact that in his human nature, or as Christ *incarnate*, he has discharged his office as high priest for us. It would take us too far afield to review all that is said in that connection in the letter to the Hebrews. But it is recapitulated there that under the Old Testament Mosaic administration, it was necessary that a high priest should do for the people what, as a result of the sinful state in which they stood, they could not do for themselves. Adam himself was at the first constituted a priest under God and enjoyed full and free communion with God. But at the Fall he lost his ability and capacity to discharge that high and holy office. Henceforth man could not have direct and unmediated access to God. His access must be through the mediation of a priest whom God appointed for that purpose. When the Mosaic system was institutionalized, and when the designated and formalized office of priest replaced the respect in which, in the preceding patriarchal age, the head of the family had performed that office, the high priest was charged with the performance of a specific and important function. It was his responsibility on the annual Day of Atonement, first to offer a sacrifice for his own sin and to sprinkle the blood of the sacrifice on the Ark of the Covenant and the mercy seat in the most holy place within the tabernacle. By doing so he acquired for himself a ceremonial holiness. Then after that, he was to offer a sacrifice for the sins of the people and sprinkle the blood of that sacrifice again on the Ark of the Covenant and the mercy seat. By that means the people also acquired a ceremonial holiness. They could, as a result, worship God through the mediation of the high priest, as they looked in faith to the promise that in due time the Messiah would come as the true and the final sacrifice for sin.

The letter to the Hebrews explains that Christ came as the antitype of all the ceremonial types that anticipated him and pointed to him in that earlier dispensation. By virtue of his once-for-all offering of himself for sin, the slate of charges against his people was wiped clean. "Christ being come an high priest ... neither by the blood of goats and calves, but by his own blood he entered in once into the holy place, having obtained eternal redemption for us" (Heb. 9:11-12). In him, all the prophecy of redemption is fulfilled.

The writer of the letter to the Hebrews is at pains to make clear in several ways the respects in which the high priesthood of Christ is superior to that of the high priest under the older Mosaic, or Levitical, administration. First, the high priests of old had to enter the most holy place of the Tabernacle once a year every year, with their repetitive sacrifice for sin. The sacrifice had to be offered over and over again, because all that it could do was provide for the people a ceremonial holiness, or deal with their ceremonial guilt before God. As the writer says, "It is not possible that the blood of bulls and goats should take away sin" (Heb. 10:4). The older ceremonies could not deal definitively with sin or remove the moral guilt under which the people stood. Only the "better sacrifice" of Christ could do that, and when he came he offered a once-for-all sacrifice that dealt definitively with all of the sin and moral guilt of his people. As a result, God could say of his people that "their sins and iniquities will I remember no more" (Heb. 10:17). The vision of the Psalmist has materialized: "As far as the east is from the west, so far hath he removed our transgressions from us" (Ps. 103:12).

At the heart of the gospel lies the remarkable fact that Christ was not only the high priest who made the definitive offering for sin, but he was himself the offering. Again the letter to the Hebrews is eloquent on the point. Indeed, the very beginning of the letter makes a declaration to that effect, before the writer goes on to work out the meaning of it in detail. He says at the beginning that it was "when he had *by himself* purged our sins, [he] sat down on the right hand of the Majesty on high" (Heb. 1:3).

While all of that illumines what Christ did as our high priest when he was in this world, the glory of the gospel revelation is that he continues that office for us now in heaven. "For Christ," the same writer says, "is not entered into the holy place made with hands ... but into heaven itself, now to appear in the presence of God for us" (Heb. 9:24).

What, then, is to be seen as the essence of his heavenly priesthood that Christ is discharging for us? That is revealed in a twofold aspect: first, his sympathy for us; and secondly, his continual intercession for us. We do not have space to spell out all of the meaning of those two aspects of our Lord's continual work for us. But in them we have both the culmination of his redemptive work on our behalf and our eternal security as his people who are joined to him.

Christ will come again in due time to receive us unto himself. Then we shall reign with him for ever. We shall in due time be more blessed with him than we are now, for it is true that things are prepared for us that we cannot at the present time imagine or contemplate. It is true that we shall be more blessed. But it is not true that we shall be more secure. For we are now secure eternally in him. That is what he has accomplished by his faithful discharge of his redemptive office. He came to save us, his people, from our sin (Matt. 1:21), and that is precisely what he has done.

The prophetic and kingly offices of Christ

The Westminster Shorter Catechism has summarized the redemptive offices of Christ in its statement that "Christ, as our Redeemer, executeth the offices of a prophet, of a priest, and of a king, both in his estate of humiliation and exaltation."[2] In the same way as we have considered the priestly office of Christ in both its earthly and its heavenly aspects, so we may reflect upon our Lord's prophetic and kingly offices.

---

[2] Westminster Shorter Catechism, Question 23.

In our present context a small number of points call for briefer comment for the light they throw on the benefits of our redemption.

First, Adam, in his capacity as vicegerent under God, was charged with the offices of prophet, priest, and king. We saw in an earlier chapter that in his capacity as prophet he was to discover, understand, and explain the meaning of the reality-environment in which he came to self-consciousness as the image of God. As a priest he was privileged to have direct communion with God, as God walked with him "in the garden in the cool of the day" (Gen. 3:8), and he was to dedicate back to God all that he learned and knew and did. As king, he was to rule over all of created reality to the glory of God. He was to "have dominion" over all things (Gen. 1:28). But the sorry reality is that our first parents repudiated their covenantal obligations by their damning assumption of autonomy from God. From that point on, they were no longer able to meet and discharge the responsibilities of their offices of prophet, priest, and king.

Given the disability of human nature that followed from Adam's Fall, the resulting situation meant that if the requirements of God in the establishment of those offices were to be satisfied it was necessary that the offices should be executed by a substitute on man's behalf. But how could that be done? In response, the glory of God's redemptive revelation is that his own Son came from his eternal reign with the Father to do precisely that. That, at its most fundamental level, is the meaning of the fact that Christ came as prophet, priest, and king. He came in those offices in order to do for us what we were obligated under God's creation covenant to do but could not do for ourselves. Christ is our substitute prophet, our substitute priest, and our substitute king.

The benefits of redemption are such, therefore, that not only is the penalty for the sins of God's people paid by the Substitute who was their priest who offered himself for them. Not only is the slate of condemnation against them under the law of God wiped clean by his substitutionary sin-bearing. Not only is their title to heaven assured on the grounds of all that their Substitute did for them. The remarkable fact also is that all of their obligations under the mandates and requirements of God's initial covenant of creation are satisfied. We need to see briefly why that is so.

The essence of the office of prophet is that of explanation. The Old Testament prophets, for example, were charged to explain God's requirements of his people, as they explained also God's charge against them for their sin. In that capacity the prophet represented God to the people. In Adam's unfallen state, his prophetic office was again essentially that of explanation, of explaining the meaning and potential of his reality-environment. An example of his doing that at the beginning is contained in his naming the animals that were brought to him for that purpose (Gen. 2:19-20). By virtue of his pristine relation with God his Creator, he was in possession of all necessary categories and principles in terms of which his explanation of things was to proceed. But at that point one of the terrible implications of his fall comes to effect. Adam's Fall meant that in the darkness of mind and ignorance that resulted he lost his understanding of the principles of explanation that God has initially communicated to him. But man's rescue in that respect also is in Christ. For Christ now discharges the office of prophet by giving us again the true principles of explanation of all things that we had lost in Adam.

That has a wide implication and application. For we have said that Christ communicates to his people the principles of explanation of all things. And the "all things" include not only those aspects of our lives that have to do with our entrance to the state of salvation that Christ's life and death has assured. It has to do also with every aspect of life and existence. The breadth of the implication should not be in any sense diminished. It means that all discovery of truth and meaning in all aspects of life depends on the principles of explanation that exist in Christ and are communicated to us by him. That has reference to all aspects of cultural progress, in science, the arts, and on all levels on which human experience and discovery can be contemplated. Nothing less than that is referenced in the apostolic statement that "in [Christ] are hid all the treasures of wisdom and knowledge" (Col. 2:3). If the conclusion may sound too broad, reflect for a moment on a simple possibility. Consider the flower that blooms in the field. It may be that, as Thomas Gray saw it, "Full many a flower is born to blush unseen,/ And waste its sweetness on the desert air."[3] Many people, from the vantage point of their particular interests, may describe the flower. They may paint it, lyricize about it, describe its material composition, or use it for purposes of adornment. But when all that is said and done, it may remain necessary to say that none of those individuals has truly known and understood the flower. For true truth about the flower has not been attained until it is known and stated that it is God's flower.

The same conclusion applies to all possibilities of truth on all levels. By the common grace of God unregenerate people, scientists for example who may claim that God does not exist, or who claim that if he exists he is irrelevant to what transpires in the world, may make true statements about the world. But such discoveries are made, not because the universe is a universe of randomness and chance as the scientist may assume, but because it is a God-created universe that operates in accordance with God-established laws. Unregenerate scientists are able to make claims to truth because in doing so they are operating, in spite of what might be their insistence to the contrary, in a world that is shot through with God-created laws of being and operation. In all things, those know truly who know God truly.

---

[3] Thomas Gray, *Elegy written in a country churchyard*, lines 55-56. (various editions).

Christ is our prophet, as the Catechism says, "in revealing to us, by his word and Spirit, the will of God for our salvation."[4] And he is our prophet also, as we have now seen, in conveying to us the principles of explanation and of meaning that we had lost in Adam's Fall. The explanation that the prophetic office of Christ provides extends to all aspects and relations relevant to our standing before God. It includes the way of salvation and the necessities of moral obligation and imperative that that implies.

Christ is our king, as he is our prophet and priest. By Adam's Fall again we lost the ability to discharge our office and responsibility of rule over all things to the glory of God. But Christ is king, and he has "made us unto our God kings and priests" (Rev. 5:10). By his common grace as we journey in this life he grants us abilities to subdue and rule over our environment and to cultivate it for purposes of our own preservation and the good of our neighbors. The common grace of God is at work in the world, by his immanent works of providence and by the administration by his Spirit, to preserve the world until the time of his appointed last day comes. That administration of his grace is in the interests of his church. For God's purposes in the history of the world is that the ordained end of the salvation of all of his elect church should be realized. It is for that purpose that we can say that God has eventuated, and that he is eventuating, all of human history in the interest of his church.

When it is said that Christ is king, we are saying that he is our substitute in that he guides us in the exercise of our kingship over the world in accordance with the purposes he has ordained. In that again he is doing for us what we were obligated to do under God's initial covenant of creation but were disabled by the Fall from doing for ourselves. But more is at issue. By reason of our redemption by Christ we are

---

[4] Westminster Shorter Catechism, Question 24.

joined to him in a vital, spiritual, and indissoluble union. We have it on the promise of his Word that he has ordained that we should reign with him. Christ has been made by the Father, "Heir of all things" (Heb. 1:2), and as he has gone to prepare an inheritance for us (Heb. 9:15), the glory of the gospel is that we whom he has redeemed will at last reign with him.

Chapter 8

The Application of Redemption: Regeneration, Justification, Sanctification

The glory of the gospel is that God has reconciled to himself his people who were "dead in trespasses and sins" (Eph. 2:1). God has intervened by his sovereign initiative in their otherwise hopeless state, and "even when we were dead in sins, [he] hath quickened us together with Christ (by grace are ye saved) and hath raised us up together, and made us sit together in heavenly places in Christ Jesus" (Eph. 2:5-6). Such is the result of what the Scriptures describe as the sovereign secret, and unsolicited regenerating work of the Holy Spirit of God in the soul of those whom Christ, in the full discharge of his messianic office, has redeemed. At issue now is the application to Christian believers of the benefits and blessings of the redemption that Christ accomplished. We shall look at some of those blessings in this chapter.

Consider the doctrine of regeneration. Questions that warrant careful meditation, many of which should usefully be considered further beyond the following discussion, have to do with the essence of the work of the Holy Spirit in regeneration; the effect of regeneration on the faculties of the soul; the respect in which the believer, as a result of regeneration, can or cannot be said to possess both an "old" or sinful nature and a "new" or regenerate nature; the sense, as a result, in which the individual is a new person; and the meaning of sin in the life of the regenerate person. A corresponding multiple of questions arise in connection with the doctrines of justification and sanctification. We shall return to them.

The preceding chapters have considered the state of man, both as created and as fallen into the state of sin. We have seen that sin is in essence the repudiation of covenantal obligations to God, but we have also seen the provision for redemption that God has set forth in his Son. And we have recognized the scriptural data that establish what we called the particularity of the atonement. Christ died to save the people whom God the Father gave him to redeem before the foundation of the world.

As we consider now the application to those for whom Christ died of the benefits of the redemption he accomplished, the redemptive office of the Holy Spirit in calling us to Christ comes into view. As the Catechism puts it, "Convincing us of our sin and misery, enlightening our minds in the knowledge of Christ, and renewing our wills, he doth persuade and enable us to embrace Jesus Christ, freely offered to us in the gospel."[1] Beyond that effectual call, the Holy Spirit continues his work of grace within us "whereby we are renewed in the whole man after the image of God, and are enabled more and more to die unto sin, and live unto righteousness."[2] We have in those statements the essence of our doctrines of regeneration and sanctification.

---

[1] Westminster Shorter Catechism, Question 31.
[2] Ibid., Question 35.

A preliminary point on the nature of the individual

We now consider in more detail what is involved in that divine work of the Holy Spirit. But we must first endeavor to gain a clear understanding of the status of the person who is thus renewed in Christ. We begin by recalling what is to be said of man as he was created. We don't recall all that was said about man as the image of God. We are interested, rather, in the fact that we do not say that man *has* a body and that he *has* a soul. Consider what would be involved if we said that. We would then be speaking of three entities. We would have, first, the man who, we would be supposing, possesses the body and the soul. Then secondly, we would have the body that he possesses. And then we would have the soul that he is said to possess. There would be those three entities, the man, the body, and the soul.

But we don't say that. We say, rather, not that man *has* a body and a soul, but that man *is* body and soul. We shall see in a moment why we make that point. In doing so, we shall refer to the manner in which the nineteenth-century theologian, Robert Dabney, looked at these same questions. As Dabney put our present point, the individual "has one consciousness, he knows that he is one indivisible personality."[3] With such a basic proposition in view, the focus of our thought falls on the one indivisible personality that the individual is. John Murray held the same view when he says, "The body is an integral part of personality."[4] The matter is stated in that form in order to bring into view an analogy of what our present doctrines require us to say about the status of the individual person. We shall refer to the implications of

---

[3] Robert L. Dabney, *Discussions: Evangelical and Theological* (London: Banner of Truth, 1967), vol. 1, 196.
[4] John Murray, *The Epistle to the Romans* (Grand Rapids: Eerdmans, 1959), vol. 1, 221.

that understanding of integral personhood for the individual in his or her regenerate and unregenerate states.

The statement we have made by analogy from the doctrine of man is preliminary to what will be said of the nature of the individual to whom the benefits of Christ's redemption are applied. So far, we have focused our thought on what man is. Now to see the application of our analogy, let us say the following. In the same way, and focusing now on a further aspect of the nature of man, we say, not that man *has* a certain nature, but that what he *is* is characterized by a certain nature. That nature, we shall see, may be an old or unregenerate nature, or it may be a new and regenerate nature. In other words, we hold carefully now to the fact that the so-called "nature" of man is simply what describes the man. The man *is* what his nature is.

We can look ahead at this early point to anticipate what we shall say in a similar way about the individual when he has been made regenerate. We shall say, consistent with our analogy, not that he *has* a new nature, but that he himself *is* "new" by virtue of the characteristics of nature that now describe him. But, as we shall see, because of the integral nature of the individual in his personhood, and because the characteristics of nature that now describe him are what they are because the Holy Spirit has endowed him with them, it is not a matter of his possessing both an "old" nature and a "new" nature. The new person in Christ is what he is simply because the characteristics of nature that now describe him are what they are. Again the man is what his nature is. The "nature" is what describes the man.

But we are running ahead of our subject. Let us look now at what it is the Holy Spirit effects in the soul by his work of regeneration. In doing so we shall have more to say about the new nature that describes the regenerate Christian man, and, in particular, about the ability of that new man to sin. The paradox exists that the true believer is a saint and yet he remains subject to the reality of indwelling sin.

The effects of regeneration on the faculties of the soul

Two things must now be said in order to hold our doctrines of regeneration and sanctification in proper perspective. First, regeneration does not involve the creation of any new faculties within the soul of the individual that did not previously exist. Second, what is involved is the endowment of the existing faculties of the soul with new abilities and capacities which, in the state of sin, they did not previously possess, and the implantation in the soul of a new disposition or principle of action. That is so, because in his regenerating work the Holy Spirit has endowed the faculties of the soul with precisely those new abilities.

Looking again at the integral personhood of the individual, and recalling that at his creation as God's image he was endowed with the faculties of mind, heart, and will, we say the following. When we considered the doctrine of sin, we saw that those faculties were disabled in ways that required us to say that the fallen individual had become the captive slave of the Devil. His mind was blinded, and he could not see and understand the things of God, his heart was turned to obey the lusts of Satan and the flesh and it was filled with a hatred of God (Rom. 1:30), and the will was weakened and was no longer the recipient of holy instructions from a holy mind and heart. The individual could not see or know or love or obey God, because he was in every sense, and in all of the faculties of his soul, enslaved to Satan and sin.

But now, when the same faculties of the soul are renewed by the regenerating work of God's Holy Spirit, there is such a radical change in their capacities and abilities that the only way to describe the person to whom it has happened is to say that he is a "new creation" (2 Cor. 5:17). Old things are passed away and all things are new. The change that the Holy Spirit effects in the soul, the endowment of new abilities and capacities within its faculties, is so radical, so completely transforming, that when the New Testament writers search for words to describe it they can only fall back on what our Lord himself said. The only way to describe what has happened is to say that the individual has been "born again." He is now something completely and radically different from what he was before.

But now we can ask the question we have anticipated, and we can see the relevance of the analogy we have raised. Again we bear in mind the integral personhood of the individual. Should we say, then, that while the regenerate person continues to possess his old nature he now has also a new nature? That, I am saying, is the very thing we can not say. As a result of regeneration, the individual is simply new. His capacities of soul are now what they were not before. They have been renewed. They are not different faculties, but they have been so transformed in their abilities that their nature is completely different.

This, it can be acknowledged, is a point of doctrine that has at times been sadly and badly misunderstood in the evangelical church. The erroneous doctrine that there is in the regenerate Christian both an old nature and a new nature is traceable to a teaching that was prominent in Plymouth Brethren circles in the mid-nineteenth century and which was given further prominence in the Scofield Bible. It has found its way into the New International Version of the Scriptures, where that translation repeatedly translates the word "flesh" as "sinful nature." It thereby preserves the false doctrine of two natures in the regenerate man. There is, moreover, a serious danger implicit in the doctrine on a very practical level. For many who hold the "two natures" doctrine do, nevertheless, acknowledge the reality of sin in the life of the Christian person. But then on that view of things sin is easily explained by saying that it is the old nature that sins and not the new nature. We shall return to that important point, but we can say immediately two things. First, sin in the regenerate person is very real. There can be no confusion about that. We who are regenerate are, in spite of our regenerate status, guilty of sin every day. But second, when we sin, it is not a matter of one of our natures sinning. It is *we* who sin. And we in our persons are guilty of sin. What we are saying is that we must not confuse in our doctrine two things that are quite distinct. The fact that the regenerate person is a "new" individual who is described by the characteristics of a "new" nature, must be kept quite distinct from the fact that that new person is still capable of sin. We shall return to that point.

Before we proceed any further, let us ask again what it is that regeneration involves. We say, to use the words of Dabney, that "it reverses the moral *habitus* [i.e. disposition] of the believer's will, prevalently [that is, that a new disposition is prevalent, or prevails, in the soul], but not at first absolutely, and that the work of progressive sanctification carries on this change.... In the carnal state, the *habitus* [or disposition] of the sinner's will is absolutely and exclusively godless. In the regenerate state it is prevalently but not completely godly. In the glorified state it is absolutely and exclusively godly."[5] The important fact is that, as we have said before, the Christian is "one indivisible personality," and it is that one person who, by virtue of his regeneration, is now disposed, but not yet absolutely, to reflect in his life and actions the perfect holiness of God. And, as Dabney has correctly stated, "The Bible is still further from saying that the renewed man has two '*natures*.'" The two natures theory, Dabney says, "flies flatly in the face of the Scriptures."[6]

In view of the importance of what has been said for the doctrine of regeneration and the sanctification that proceeds from it, a further observation might be noted. Referring to those who hold the "two natures" theory, Dabney says: "We challenge them to produce a text from the New Testament where it is said that regeneration is the implantation of a 'new *nature*' beside the old; or that the renewed man has two

---

[5] Dabney, *Discussions*, vol. 1, 196ff.
[6] Ibid., 194.

hostile '*natures*,' or any such language.... Paul ... teaches that the renewed man (one man and one nature still) is imperfect, having two principles of volition mixed in the motives even of the same act; but he does not teach that he has become 'two men,' or has 'two natures' in him. Paul's idea is, that man's one nature, originally wholly sinful, is by regeneration made imperfectly holy, but progressively so.... [The doctrine of the two natures in man] contradicts the consciousness of every Christian, even the most unlearned; for just as surely as he has one consciousness, he knows that he is one indivisible personality, and that he is one agent and has only *one will*, swayed indeed by mixed and diverse motives."[7]

John Murray, again recognizing the integral personality of the individual, makes the same point by saying that "the old man is the unregenerate man; the new man is the regenerate man created in Christ Jesus unto good works. It is no more feasible to call the believer a new man and an old man, than it is to call him a regenerate man and an unregenerate. And neither is it warranted to speak of the believer as having in him the old man and the new man."[8]

Sin in the life of the Christian

A paradox describes the Christian's life. He is a saint and yet he is a sinner. He is a saint because by the regenerating work of the Spirit of which we have spoken he has been set apart for God. In the words of the apostle to the Colossians, it is said of such people, "The Father ... hath delivered us from the power of darkness, and hath translated us into the kingdom of his dear Son" (Col. 1:12-13). Peter says that the new-born person has been "called out of darkness into his marvellous light" (1 Peter 2:9). For that reason the apostolic letters

---

[7] Ibid., 192-96.
[8] John Murray, *Principles of Conduct* (Grand Rapids: Eerdmans, 1957), 218-19.

frequently address their readers as "saints" (Eph. 1:1; Phil. 1:1; Col. 1:2). But the reality of the Christian life is that the Christian sins. Of that there is no doubt, and the witness of the Scriptures to the fact, as well as that of the sanctified conscience of the believer, deserves careful reflection and meditation. The well-known argument of the apostle Paul in the seventh chapter of his letter to the Romans, where he wrestles with the reality of sin, is eloquent testimony to the fact. We properly ask, how can that be so, in the light of what has been said regarding the renewing work of God's Holy Spirit in the soul?

The Psalmist has underlined the seriousness of the question. For our sin does not consist only in the actions and the imaginations of the heart of which we are conscious. It does not consist only in those aspects of behavior that the renewed conscience knows is offensive to the holiness and the preceptive will of God. The Psalmist prays also, "Who can understand his errors? Cleanse thou me from my secret faults" (Ps. 19:12). By his "secret faults," or secret sins, David undoubtedly has in mind not simply sins that are hidden from other people or those that we may try to, or be able to, cover over as we present ourselves to the world and even to the church. The secret sins refer also to the sins of which we ourselves are not aware. "Who can understand his errors?" David asks. That in itself may sound paradoxical. But consider the import of it.

It is a part of the Christian life and experience that as the sanctifying work of the Spirit of God in the soul progresses, the Christian believer will become progressively aware of the meaning of sin. We may put that in very practical terms. The Christian will often come to understand that what has not, at an early stage of life, appeared as sin, will in due time be seen as being, on the level of thought, behavior, and indulgence, sin that must be avoided and done away with. That is the nature of the Holy Spirit's ministry of sanctification. It involves in the Christian's life a developing sensitivity to the sinfulness of sin. An old Puritan author, Ralph Venning, writing in 1669, speaks eloquently of the sinfulness of sin in his valuable book, *The Plague of Plagues*.[9]

Consider further what has been said regarding the meaning of regeneration. It does not involve the creation of new faculties. It involves the endowment of the existing faculties with new capacities and new abilities. The regenerate person can now see things with his mind that he could never have seen before. He finds that his heart is now inclined to seek after God where before he hated God. And he finds within him a new ability, a new strength of will, to obey God. He now loves the law of God that previously he hated, and he wants to do the will of God. He does not have a new nature added to an old nature. The person is what the characteristics of his nature describe him to be. His nature is simply, to quote Dabney again, "that aggregate of permanent characteristic attributes [that describe] the quality of a person."[10]

But now we face the reality of sin. When we say that the regenerate person is a new person, characterized by a wholly different nature from what previously described him, we nevertheless acknowledge that that person sins. How, then, is that to be explained? We don't explain it by saying that it is the old nature that sins. We say, rather, that it is the *person* who sins. The individual in his integral personhood is guilty of the sin. Because it is the *person* who sins, it is the *person* who is responsible for the sin. Our doctrine does not in any way minimize the reality or the seriousness of sin. It emphasizes the seriousness of sin.

But what, more precisely, are we to understand as the old *habitus* or principle of action that can and does at times pull the believer into occasions of sin? It is simply that old habits, old preferences, and old alignments can and do from time to time raise their head and remind the believer of the old

---

[9] Ralph Venning, *The Plague of Plagues* (London: Banner of Truth, 1965).
[10] Dabney, op. cit., 196.

pleasures of sin. For that reason, sin in the life of the believer is explained, first, by the pressures and temptations to sin that come from outside of himself; and secondly, by the capacity to respond to that by the habits of earlier life whose ingrained residence in the soul is being progressively displaced.

The scriptural data require us to state that last point as clearly as possible. As to the proper characterization of sin in the life of the believer, the apostle James has clarified for us that "every man is tempted, when he is drawn away of his own lust, and enticed" (James 1:14). What are we to say of what James has referred to as that remaining "lust" in the renewed person? It is well known that the Roman Catholic church, consistent with the deliverances of the Council of Trent, insists that the lust we have in view, or what it refers to as concupiscence, is not in itself sinful, though it may well lead to sin.[11] But that doctrinal claim has been rigorously denied by the Reformed theology from which the Tridentine Council dissented. The concupiscence, the remaining lust, in the renewed person is itself sinful, as the Westminster doctrine on the point maintains: "The corruption of nature ... *itself* and all the motions thereof, are truly and properly sinful."[12] What is at issue, then, is that what we have seen Dabney refer to as the "old *habitus*," the old principle of action, or the old disposition from which the Christian believer is not yet wholly free is itself sinful and that it is capable of rising and coming to expression in the entertainment of sin.

We can put that differently in the language of the seventeenth-century Puritan theologian, John Owen. In his treatise, *A Discourse Concerning the Holy Spirit*, Owen addresses the reality of sin in the life of the truly regenerate person. "One thing yet remains to be cleared," Owen says, "that there may

---

[11] See William Cunningham, *Historical Theology* (Edinburgh: Banner of Truth, 1960), vol.1, 528-42.
[12] Westminster Confession of Faith, VI, 5.

be no mistake in this matter; and this is, that in those who are constantly inclined and disposed unto all the acts of a heavenly, spiritual life, there are yet remaining contrary dispositions and inclinations also. There are yet in them inclinations and dispositions to sin, *proceeding from the remainders of a contrary habitual principle*.... This yet continueth in them, inclining them unto evil and all that is so, according to the power and efficacy that is remaining unto it in various degrees."[13] Owen's argument is, as we have seen, reflected in that of Dabney. And what Owen refers to as the "contrary habitual principle" is again a reference to what is described in the Scriptures as indwelling sin. "This," Owen says, "the Scripture calls ... the 'sin that dwelleth in us.'"[14]

The condition we have to address has been explained by John Murray in terms similar to those we have adopted when he says that "the believer is a new man, a new creature, but he is a new man not yet made perfect. Sin dwells in him, and he still commits sin. He is necessarily the subject of progressive renewal ... but that progressive renewal ... is not to be conceived of as the progressive crucifixion of the old man."[15] The Christian is a new person, characterized and described by a new nature, but his faculties of soul, while they have been renewed with new endowments in the manner we have seen, have not yet been made perfect. They are still capable of being deceived by sin, by the allurements of the world, by old habits and indulgences, and by the subtleties of the Devil and his angels. That remaining ability to be led astray into sin by old habits and old imaginations has been referred to in doctrinal terms as "indwelling sin." It is what Paul wrote about so eloquently in the seventh chapter of his letter to the Romans in his description of the life of the regenerate man.

---

[13] John Owen, *Discourse Concerning the Holy Spirit*, in *The Works of John Owen* (London: Banner of Truth, 1965), Vol. 3, 488, italics added.
[14] Idem.
[15] John Murray, *Principles of Conduct*, 219.

Sin dwells with the Christian because while his faculties have been renewed in principle, their transformation to the image of the holiness of God has not yet been perfected. Here, at this very important point of the Christian's practical experience, is a mystery, the mystery that the new man in Christ, the person who is now described by a new nature, is capable of sin and does, in fact, sin. Why, we have to ask again, is that so?

The answer is that God in his eternal wisdom, while he has implanted within us those new abilities of soul, and while he has so renewed the faculties of our souls with new abilities and capacities that we can only be described by saying that our nature is "new," he has not yet transformed us to the state of perfection of holiness that we shall one day attain. We are still in the body. The body, we have seen, is an integral part of our personality. It is to be said of the bodily aspect, as it is to be said of the aspect of soul of the individual, that it is no longer controlled and conditioned by sin. But the body is capable of actions that are sinful. Our faculties can still be confused and led astray by Satan and sin. We are new people, and one day we shall be perfect. But that day is not yet. God in his wisdom has left us in this world to live through the experience of seeing our own selves progressively transformed to become at last fully consistent with the new persons in Christ that he has already made us to be. We can fall into sin, and we are responsible for sin, alarmingly responsible. But sin can no longer reign over us. And as John has said in his first epistle, when we realize who we are, then by reason of that we cannot consent to continue in sin (1 John 3:6, 9).

What has been said raises a final point in connection with sin in the life of the believer. That question is to be considered against the facts and meaning of the believer's true identity. The Christian's life is possible, we shall go on to see more fully, because such an individual is now joined to Christ. That mysterious union is what it is because Christ has sent his Spirit into residence in the soul of the believer. As the eighteenth-century evangelical, Henry Scougal, put it, the grace of regeneration establishes "the life of God in the soul of man."[16]

It is not possible to describe or define the Christian person except by defining him as joined to Christ. But if, as is demonstrably the case, that vital and spiritual union exists, then we must say that every action of such a person is an action by a person who is joined to Christ. If that person rejoices, it is the rejoicing of a person who is joined to Christ. If that person sins, it is the sinning of a person who is joined to Christ. No longer does there exist between God and the individual a distanced relation of unreconcilable identity. The true believer is not now left to himself as a distanced antagonist of God. We can say nothing less than that the Sprit of God is within him and, with the apostle Paul, "Christ liveth in me" (Gal. 2:20). But the person who now stands in that high estate sins. Of course he sins. The fact we have to face is that when that person sins it is a person who is joined to Christ that sins. That is the fact from which there can be no escape.

Every thought and action of the true Christian believer, then, is the thought and action of a person who is joined to Christ. The Christian person does not, and cannot, live independently of Christ to whom he is now joined. If that were not so, there would be no point in the apostle's admonition, "Grieve not the holy Spirit of God, by whom ye are sealed unto the day of redemption" (Eph. 4:30). But because the Christian is who he is, God by his Spirit will frustrate his very attempt to continue in sin. As the apostle John put it, "Whosoever is born of God doth not commit sin; for his seed remaineth in him; and he cannot sin [that is, he cannot consent to continue in sin], because he is born of God" (1 John 3:9). It is a remarkable fact of God's ministry to his saints that he frustrates their desires to leave him and to fall continually into sin. As John Owen puts it, "he ... stops the course of sin."

---

[16] Henry Scougal, *The Life of God in the Soul of Man* (Harrisonburg. VA.: Sprinkle Publications, 1986).

Observe how Owen makes the point. "When lust hath conceived, and is ready to bring forth – when the soul lies at the brink of some iniquity – he [God] gives in seasonable help, relief, deliverance, and safety. Here lies a great part of the care and faithfulness of Christ towards his poor saints. He will not suffer them to be worried with the power of sin, nor to be carried out unto ways that shall dishonour the gospel, or fill them with shame and reproach, and so render them useless in the world; but he steps in with the saving relief and assistance of his grace, stops the course of sin, and makes them in himself more than conquerors. And this assistance lies under the promise, 1 Cor. 10:13."[17]

But when all that is said, the truth remains that in the Christian believer's flirtation with sin, God may, and as occasion warrants he does, withdraw "the light of his countenance."[18] That causes the believer's loss of joy, comfort, and usefulness, and effectiveness in his service for the Lord who has saved him.

The loss of the face of God, its causes and remedies

The poverty of soul that is consequent on God's "hiding himself," to recall the expressive phrase of Owen, is well known to the serious believer. "What peace, I pray, is there to a soul while God hides himself ...?"[19] Such a condition, he

---

[17] John Owen, "The Nature and Power of Indwelling Sin," in *Works* (Edinburgh: Banner of Truth, 1967), vol. 6, 277. This statement of Owen is to be set against his comment on the same text, 1 Cor. 10:13, in his essay, "On temptation": "Though there be a sufficiency of grace provided for all the *elect*, that they shall by no temptation fall utterly from God, yet it would make any gracious heart to tremble, to think what dishonour to God, what scandal to the gospel, what woful darkness and disquietness they may bring upon their own souls, though they perish not" op. cit., in *Works*, vol. 6, 116-17.

[18] Westminster Confession, XI, 5.

[19] John Owen, "Of the Mortification of Sin in Believers," in *Works* (Edinburgh: Banner of Truth, 1967), vol. 6, 53.

has learned, follows from the sin of belief and behavior that is consistent with a previous status and character. The poet and hymn-writer of the eighteenth-century evangelical awakening, William Cowper, has given eloquent expression to what is involved when the believer loses the light of the face of God:

> O! for a closer walk with God,
> A calm and heavenly frame;
> A light that shines upon the road
> That leads me to the lamb!
>
> Where is the blessedness I knew
> When first I saw the Lord?
> Where is the soul-refreshing view
> Of Jesus and his word?

Cowper's plea was raised against the reality of the unrest and discomfort, the anguish and the temporary barrenness of soul that is for a time bereft of the comfort of the realized presence of God:

> Return, O holy dove, return,
> Sweet messenger of rest;
> I hate the sins that made thee mourn,
> And drove thee from my breast.[20]

But why should the "loss of the face of God" be at all possible for the truly born-again child of God? First, subjectively, it is clear that the condition of which we have spoken is traceable primarily and paramountly to a weakening of prayer in the Christian life. Adequate guidance is available in the Word of God as to the necessity and urgency, the proper

---

[20] William Cowper, *Walking with God*, in Donald Davie, ed., *The New Oxford Book of Christian Verse* (Oxford: Oxford University Press, 1981), 198.

forms, and the sanctifying effectiveness of the believer's consistent life of prayer. How little we know of what is required of us in prayer in order that God will be glorified and that we ourselves will grow in both our consciousness of the faith and our conformity to his image in Christ to which we are called. And how little we know experimentally of the sanctifying contributions of prayer as we purport to progress through this short, uncertain life and earthly pilgrimage to the glory that God has prepared for those who love him. Should not our prayer be for forgiveness for our laxity and lack of diligence at this very initial and basic point?

Consider the anguish of the spouse in the Song of Solomon: "I sought him whom my soul loveth; I sought him, but I found him not" (Song of Sol. 3:1). The beloved had withdrawn. Should we not show the same diligence in wanting his company, in seeking him, and rejoicing again in the discovery of him and the comfort of his grace?

Secondly, that subjective issue aside, we must say objectively that the cause of God's hiding his face from us is that we are too readily delinquent, as we shall see again below, in pursuing the means of grace he has provided for us. We say that we have been called into the fellowship of his church, but we are hesitant to understand what his church is, and what are the terms of the covenant of grace by which it stands. We have covenanted to fulfill certain obligations that we assumed at entry to membership of the church in its visible aspect, but we too often regard the church as a societal entity, the voluntariness of whose membership excuses us from its more rigorous and insistent demands. We are saved as God brings us to faith individually. We are individually responsible and accountable to God our maker, judge, and redeemer. But we too readily allow that individuality to give us cause to act individualistically within the church, to the loss of the demands of the solidarity to which we have been called and admitted.

We are too often reluctant to submit to the consistent

search of the Word of God and to hear that Word preached. We too easily forget to ponder the love of the saints. We have neglected a true understanding of the grace of the sacraments. We too readily import into the church the thought-forms and the behavior-norms of the world. We bend to the culture of the world and fail to realize that by his saving grace God has introduced us to a distinctively different culture, the culture of the church. We fail to think out under the guidance of God's Word what are the necessary marks of that distinctive culture. We know that the church is in the world to bear witness to the good news of the gospel of grace, but we fail to be alarmed at the fact that the world is in the church. In short, we are reluctant to be conformed to the mandates of the biblical data regarding the form, the sacraments, the discipline, and the purity of the church of God of which we are privileged to have been made a part.

The justification of the sinner

Between the Holy Spirit's work of regeneration at the beginning of the application of redemption and the sanctification that he will accomplish in us as he conducts us to glory is the remarkable act of God's justification of the sinner. We mean by justification the declarative act of God by which he declares the sinner to be righteous. It is a "forensic" act, where the word and concept of "forensic" relates to our status in relation to law, in this case the law of God. God's statement, on grounds that we shall inspect in a moment, that the sinner is now just or righteous, is a statement that, so far as that sinner is concerned, all of the demands of God's law have been met and satisfied. God can and does make that statement because, in the case of those whom Christ redeemed and for whom, therefore, such a statement is true, the sinner is regarded as just and righteous because Christ has acted as his substitute. We must work out the meaning of that more fully.

Why, it can be asked, does the sinner come to Christ in

repentance and faith? The answer is because the Holy Spirit of God brings the sinner to Christ. But it is precisely that movement of faith towards Christ that we must understand. At this point again, the preaching and teaching of the evangelical church has not been uniform in its statement and belief. We speak in our churches of Christians being "born again." But are we properly to say that one is born again because he has faith in Christ? Our answer must be that such a statement does not reflect the biblical doctrine.

It is not true to say that one is born again because he has faith in Christ. The precise opposite is true. One comes to faith in Christ only because he has been born again. Regeneration is prior to faith. No person can come to Christ unless and until the Holy Spirit has created new life within him, because up to that time he is, as Paul said, "dead in trespasses and sins" (Eph. 2:1). And of course a dead person cannot do anything. He is simply dead. "No man can come to me," our Lord said in his discourse on his identity as the bread of life, "except the Father which hath sent me draw him" (John 6:44). That is clarified in the record of Paul's meeting with the women by the river at Philippi. Lydia at that time came to faith in Christ. But it is not said that she opened her heart to Christ. She is described, to the contrary, as one "whose heart the Lord opened" (Acts 16:14). The regenerating awakening of the sinner and the opening of the sinner's heart to believe in Christ is there displayed as the sovereign work of God.

But what is the ground on which God can declare that the sinner who comes to him and expresses repentance and faith in Christ is at that point "just" or "justified" and "righteous"? One is "just" only when his relation to the law of God is what it ought to be. And that can be said to be true of the sinner only as Christ's perfect relation to the law of God is placed to the sinner's account. The only ground for God's declarative statement of justification is that provided by the substitutionary obedience of Christ. When we say that we are justified by faith we understand that the *efficient cause* of our salvation is the grace of God; the *meritorious cause* is the death of Christ; and our faith is the *instrumental cause*. The repentance and faith by which we turn to Christ are themselves the gifts that Christ purchased for us in his perfect obedience and death. "By grace are ye saved through faith," Paul has explained, "and that not of yourselves; it is the gift of God" (Eph. 2:8).

In his statement of justification God declares the repentant sinner righteous because the righteousness of Christ is imputed to him. In that, we have the great evangelical doctrine of double imputation. The sinner's sin is imputed to Christ, and Christ's righteousness is imputed to the sinner (2 Cor. 5:21). That declarative, forensic statement of God is to be seen as a remarkable act and provision of divine grace.

"God," Paul stated to the Romans, must be "just and the justifier of him which believeth in Jesus" (Rom. 3:26). The justice of God is maintained in three respects in the act that declares the sinner to be righteous. First, by virtue of the substitutionary redemptive work of Christ, the demands of God's holy wrath against sin are satisfied. "There is therefore now no condemnation to them which are in Christ Jesus" (Rom. 8:1). Second, as God himself must be "just," "the judgment of God is," as Turretin puts it, "according to truth."[21] That means that what God says is true and must of necessity be true. Because he is eternally righteous he cannot lie. If, therefore, God says that the sinner is righteous, the sinner must, in fact, be righteous. But how can that be so? The sinner is a sinner. And it is only because, and after, he is turned to Christ that he is declared righteous.

The fact is that in order for God to *declare* that the sinner is righteous, he actually *constitutes* him righteous. God first of all actually gives to a sinner a righteousness that the sinner did not of himself possess. God does that by giving to the sinner the *forensic righteousness* of Christ. That is at the heart of the divinely ordered act of justification. When God in that way

---

[21] Turretin, *Institutes of Elenctic Theology*, vol. 2, 647.

constitutes the sinner righteous, the sinner is then said to possess *constitutive righteousness*. How is that possible, we may ask? The answer is that God gives to the sinner the righteousness of Christ and it is thereby the sinner's own possession. That is what we mean by saying that the righteousness of Christ is imputed to the sinner.

Turretin observes: "God cannot show favor to, nor justify anyone without a perfect righteousness. For since the judgment of God is according to truth, he cannot pronounce anyone just who is not really just.... By the righteousness and obedience of one, Christ, we are constituted righteous (Rom. 5:19).... Justification takes place on account of the suretyship of Christ and the payment made for us by him."[22]

But the righteousness of God in this remarkable transaction is maintained in a third way. To summarize, God is righteous in declaring the sinner righteous, first, because the demands of his holy justice have been satisfied; secondly, because the sinner has been given the righteousness of Christ and thereby possesses a constitutive righteousness; and now thirdly, because the sinner's guilt has been given to Christ. Just as God cannot declare the sinner righteous until he *is* righteous by imputation, so God cannot declare his Son guilty until his Son *is* guilty. God has in fact declared his Son guilty because of sin – not his own sin, but our sin. That was so, because God laid the guilt of our sin upon his own Son when the Son gave his life for us. God punished sin in Christ because he transferred our guilt to him. The remarkable fact of redemption is that God punished One who was guilty, not of his own sin, but of ours. R. C. Sproul has rightly said, "The Son willingly bore, for his people, sins that are imputed or transferred to him. Here is imputation with a vengeance – indeed divine vengeance."[23]

---

[22] Ibid., 647, 651, 653.
[23] R. C. Sproul, *Faith Alone: The Evangelical Doctrine of Justification* (Grand Rapids: Baker Books, 1995), 104.

The genius of the Reformation theology is the rediscovery of the biblical doctrine that salvation is by grace alone through faith alone in Christ alone. But the testimony of the church has not always held securely to that statement of faith. From time to time movements have appeared that have blunted the edge of truth by claiming that justification is by "obedient faith," or "persevering faith." The introduction of the adjective before "faith" has tended to introduce to the doctrine of justification the necessity of works of obedience as a ground of justification. In the last day, at the day of judgment, one's final justification will turn, it is then being said, on the works of obedience that have been performed during the believer's journey in this life.

But all such doctrine evades and contradicts the biblical statement that one's justification before God turns simply, only, and completely on the once-for-all forensic statement of God at the point in time at which the righteousness of Christ is imputed to the repentant sinner. At the last great day, those who, by virtue of their regeneration and their justification, have been joined to Christ in an indissoluble union will be more blessed and more happy. But they will not be more justified. Justification – the doctrine must be securely held, and the implications of the truth lived out – is a once-for-all statement made possible by the grace of God set forth for sinners in Christ.

The process and means of sanctification

The Christian's sanctification began in the sovereign, unsolicited, regenerating work of the Holy Spirit in the soul. It is in the first place, to use the very expressive language of John Murray, "definitive."[24] By that we mean that by virtue of his regeneration the sinner is definitively, once-and-for-all, set

[24] John Murray, *The Collected Writings of John Murray* (Edinburgh: Banner of Truth, 1977), vol. 2, 277.

apart as holy for God. He is separated definitively from the slavery to the old life of sin and the sinful state in which he previously lived. The translation from the old life to the new has been done once-for-all. It is a definitive translation from the old realm of sin, condemnation, and death to the new realm of righteousness, justification, and life.

But sanctification is also to be understood as that sovereign work of the Holy Spirit within the regenerate person by which he is progressively transformed in all parts of his life and thoughts and actions to consistency with the holiness of God. Sanctification, the process of making the person progressively holy, is the work that God effects and communicates to the individual believer on the grounds of the finished work and substitutionary atonement of Christ. When we discussed in an earlier chapter the redemptive offices of the Persons of the Godhead, we saw that the Holy Spirit agreed and committed himself to apply the benefits of Christ's redemption to those for whom Christ died. The Spirit undertook that in doing so he would infallibly conduct them to glory. In order to do that, the Holy Spirit calls them to Christ and accomplishes in them the work of progressively conforming them to the image of the holiness that God has displayed in Christ. It is that process that we refer to as progressive sanctification. There are a number of things we should say about it.

First, God, by the ministry of his Holy Spirit, is sovereign in the Christian's sanctification. God makes Christ to be to the Christian believer, "wisdom and righteousness, and sanctification, and redemption" (1 Cor. 1:30). The full-orbed meaning of what God has purposed for the church that he redeemed in Christ is summed up by saying that against our ignorance, guilt, pollution, and misery Christ is made our wisdom and righteousness and sanctification and redemption. The compass of what God has purposed and guaranteed to us is wide and deep and will consummate at last in our perfect entrance to eternal glory.

When we say that God, by his Spirit, is sovereign in our sanctification we are saying quite simply that we rely on the covenantal promise of God that he will complete the work that he has begun (Phil. 1:6). Our redemption is a covenantal redemption that rests for its security on the oath of faithfulness that God has sworn. When we read, as Paul said to the Thessalonians, that "this is the will of God, even your sanctification" (I Thes. 4:3) we are entitled to see in that more than a statement that it is the *preceptive* will of God that we should be sanctified. We should see also that it is his *decretive* will that we should be sanctified. For that reason he will, by the ministry of his Holy Spirit, deal with us in such a way that we shall be brought at last to the perfection of holiness that he has decreed we should achieve as his redeemed people.

Second, while we have said that our sanctification is all the sovereign work of God by his Holy Spirit, we must say that from another perspective the work of sanctification is our work. By that we mean that because we are the new people in Christ Jesus that we have explained the regenerate person to be, we are responsible to pursue the means of grace that God has provided to us and to progress thereby in the realization of holiness. We are admonished and required to "work out [our] salvation" (Phil 2:12), and to "give diligence to make [our] calling and election sure" (2 Peter 1:10). There are, we must see from the Scriptures, two sides to what we can and should do in order to achieve that progress.

We should note in that connection that because we are new people by his grace, and because we are no longer dead in sin but are alive to God, we now have abilities to work towards holiness that we did not previously possess or understand. We therefore work towards holiness, without which, the writer to the Hebrews has said, "no man shall see the Lord" (Heb. 12:14). The two sides of our working as redeemed people can be referred to as the positive use of the means of sanctifying grace, on the one hand, and the work of mortifying our sinful proclivities and inclinations on the other.

We can say that there will be no progress in sanctification unless there is progress in the mortification of sin. But we do not say that we should set about mortifying the flesh in our own strength. Rather, there opens here again the wonder and the glory of what God has done to us and for us. We are told that if we *"through the Spirit* mortify the deeds of the body, [we] shall live" (Rom. 8:13). We are never alone now that we have been joined to Christ. His Spirit will never leave us, but will minister to us and call us repeatedly to be aware of his presence and his working in our lives.

But what are we to say if, as is so often the case, we as Christian people are careless and delinquent in pursuing the means of grace that are designed to minister to our sanctification? At that point we see again the sovereignty of the Holy Spirit. Hebrews 12 is eloquent on the fact that if we are delinquent, God in his providence will deal with us in such a way by his Holy Spirit that we will be aware of his discipline in our lives. It is the work of the Holy Spirit to exercise that discipline and the chastisement that goes along with it. If we are his people, he will do in us and for us what he has already guaranteed to the Father and the Son that he will accomplish.

What, then, are the means of grace to which we should attend and which we should cultivate? They are more extensive, and have been more lavishly provided for us than we can refer to at length at this time. They take up primarily the Holy Spirit's use of the Word of God to educate us and to mold us and to lead us into progressively higher realizations of his will for us. Our Lord himself prayed to the Father for us and said, "Sanctify them through thy truth; thy word is truth" (John 17:17). The means of grace include our attention to the privilege of not only reading the Word of God, but reflecting and meditating upon it, and in welcoming the conviction of the Holy Spirit as he communicates to us the meaning and the relevance of it. He has said to us: "I stand at the door and knock; if any man hear my voice, and open the door, I will come in to him, and will sup with him, and he with me" (Rev.

3:20). He makes that statement, not to the unregenerate sinner whose heart is dead to the things of God, but to us who have the new life that gives us the privilege and responsibility of opening our heart to him again and again. The means of sanctifying grace include also the attendance to the preaching of the Word, the privilege of fellowship with God's people who, with us, are joined to him in Christ.

Some of the implications of these doctrinal realities for the life and walk of the Christian will be addressed in the final chapter that follows.

Chapter 9

The Christian in the Church and in the World

The sense of God and the seed of religion are indelible in the human soul. That is inherent in the fact that by virtue of his creation man is the image of God. The sense of God, the awareness that *God is*, and the conviction that man is under obligation to God, rise uncalled from the recesses of human consciousness. From the imperatives of their demands there is no escape. They carry with them the testimony that man is a religious being. He must of necessity worship either the true God of whom he is consciously aware or he will worship an idol. That necessity is born in the very character of his created and derivative personhood. The idols he makes in his own image may be material, possessions that form a part of the structure of culture, or they may be things of the mind or lusts of the flesh. What we may call the religiousness of man accordingly points to either a godly religion, in which the true God is the center of human affection and conduct, or a godless religion. In the latter case, one's affection and conduct are oriented on the idols and falsehoods of his own creation or on what is culled from the context of the surrounding society and culture. That amounts in its deepest significance to the worship of oneself. For that is the essence of what characterizes the estrangement from God that sin connotes. It was the false assertion of autonomy from God that constituted our first parents' fall, and the claim to human autonomy continues and determines sinful action and commitment. Human personhood is such that man will either live as under the law of God, or he will be a law unto himself.

In the preceding chapters we have considered a number of questions and issues that come under the heading of a theology of the Christian faith. Theology, we noted, is the formulated system of belief that comes from the study of what God has revealed and which explains our relation to him. It is a human enterprise that responds to God's revelation. Now at this final point of our study we reflect on the relation between the system of Christian truth as we have looked at its essential outlines and the necessity of a religious response to God. For true religion is concerned with our living out before God the implications of the revelation he has made.

What, then, is Christian religion? We have said that human life is necessarily religious in one way or another, either godly or godless. If that is so, then Christian religion is that form and manner of life that is oriented on belief in, obedience to, and worship of the one true God whose self-revelation has been clearly expressed in Christ whom he sent into the world. We have looked at adequate length at the meaning and purpose of his coming. If, as has been said, life is essentially religious, true religion is expressed in a life that is determined and structured by the imperatives that the worship of the true God demands. True religion is life that is lived, with all consciousness and deliberation, in the presence of God.

We may draw out the implications of that conclusion in the following way. The presence of true religion in the Christian's life comes to expression on three levels: first, in the character and form of his or her own life that seeks progressive conformity to the law of holiness that God has set forth; second, in the relations the Christian is privileged to enjoy, and which bear positively on the formation of his life style, as a member of the church that God in Christ has called into being; and third, in the relations the Christian conducts in and with the world in which he is called to bear witness to the truth of God's revelation.

The Christian and personal responsibility

A moment's reflection on the doctrines we have looked at and their significance for life evokes from the Christian conscience the unspoken answer to the question of the apostle Peter: "What manner of persons ought ye to be?" (2 Peter 3:11). What, in other words, is, or should be, the true believer's response to the revelation that God has made of the truth as it is declared in his Son Christ Jesus? Peter's question arose in the context of his statement that "the day of the Lord will come as a thief in the night ... [and] ... all these things shall be dissolved." That is precisely the Christian's principal and motivating concern. For the Christian, we have said, is an eschatological person, one who lives in the light of the expectation of the final and complete fulfillment of all of God's redemptive promises. The Christian understands that it is the purpose of God that "in the dispensation of the fullness of times he might gather together in one all things in Christ, both which are in heaven, and which are on earth; even in him" (Eph. 1:10). Christ has gone "to prepare a place" for his people, and he will come again "to receive them unto himself" (John 14:2-3).

In the light of that, true religion for the Christian involves belief, obedience, and worship – belief of the truth, obedience to the demands of the truth, and worship of the God of all truth. The Christian's whole-souled commitment to the truth of God's revelation is implicit in what has been said in the preceding chapters. We recall the essence of our doctrinal development and crystallize its meaning in the following definition. A Christian is a person who, by the sovereign, gracious, regenerating work of God's Holy Spirit, has been brought to saving faith in Jesus Christ, and whom God, according to his purpose, has joined to Christ in an unmerited but actual and indissoluble union, reconciling the sinner to himself and granting him, by adoption in Christ, a right to all the graces and privileges of the sons of God. What, we are now asking, inevitably follows from that for the Christian life and his walk in the faith?

Beyond belief lies obedience. A focus on Christian obedience takes up a threefold category of understanding. First, what is it to which obedience is, or must be, directed? Second, what is to be said of the identity of the Christian person whose obedience is contemplated. And third, what abilities to obey does the Christian possess?

The object of Christian obedience is the law of God as that has been clearly set forth in its moral aspect in the Scriptures. The objective is stated in that form because of the need to understand the meaning of the law of God, first as it was given in the earlier form of administration of God's covenant of grace, and now as it remains as the rule of life for God's people. In the Mosaic administration the law of God as it was then inscripturated was given in its ceremonial, civil or judicial, and moral aspects. It has become common practice to refer to the ceremonial law, the civil or judicial law, and the moral law. A larger study of the law than can engage us at present would make it clear that the moral law as given through Moses was in its essence a republication or a rearticulation of the law of righteousness as God gave it to Adam at the beginning. For when Adam's privilege of direct communion with God was expanded to that of God's walking with him "in the garden in the cool of the day" (Gen. 3:8), God communicated to him the necessary principles of understanding work, worship, marriage, family and social arrangements, and the Sabbath. Those principles were subsequently written for our guidance in the Ten Commandments. Moreover, in the contents and structure of the ceremonial and the civil law the moral law came to its institutional expression. The essence of the moral law is expressed there in operative and ethically demanding terms.

The ceremonial law refers to that set of institutional arrangements that regulated the Israelites' forms of worship and the sacrifices that were essential to it. It included laws having to do with clean and unclean persons and things and the requirements related to the sacramental ordinances, notably the Passover and circumcision, in that earlier form of administration. That complex system of legal requirements contained many features that anticipated and pointed to the coming of the promised Messiah who would provide the definitive sacrifice for sin. It brought before God's people a system of types of the Christ who would come. But now that the Son of God has come into the world as Jesus Christ, he is the fulfillment of all that was promised under that earlier system. He is the antitype of all of the Old Testament types. He is the true High Priest, whose perfect once-for-all sacrifice of himself has done away with the repetitive earthly priests who, at their best and in their highest calling, made sacrifices every day and every year. The High Priest at that earlier time was permitted to enter only once a year into the most holy place in the tabernacle where the Ark of the Covenant stood, and by sprinkling the blood of sacrifice upon the Ark he made atonement for his own sin and the sins of the people. But now Christ has "by himself purged our sins" (Heb. 1:3) by his giving himself as the "Lamb of God" (John 1:29), and in doing so he has reconciled us to God. Now, as the reward for his faithful discharge of his covenantal engagement, he has "sat down on the right hand of the Majesty on high" (Heb. 1:3). The ceremonial law has thus been fulfilled in Christ and its demands and ceremonies have passed away.

The Christian holds to the sanctity and perpetuity of the moral law of God. But he does not holds to the sanctity and perpetuity of the institutional structures in which that moral law first came to expression. Not only has the ceremonial law passed away by reason of the fulfillment of its demands in Christ, but the civil law also no longer has binding force in the continuity of its institutions. The Westminster Confession of Faith observes judiciously in that connection: "To them also [God's people under the Old Testament administration] he [God] gave sundry judicial laws, which expired together with the state of that people, not obliging any other now, *further than the general equity thereof may require*."[1] The penal sanctions of the Old Testament civil law no longer apply in and with their earlier rigor. There is good reason why we quite properly do not now stone to death the woman who commits adultery. But the principles "of general equity," or the principles of right behavior that are implicit in the old civil law, continue to inform, or should inform, our own civil legislation. Numerous examples could be given. We don't place fences or parapets around the roofs of our houses as a protection against falling, but we build fences around our swimming pools for the same reason.

But the third aspect of the law, the moral law that God gave at the beginning and republished in the Ten Commandments, remains the rule of life. That is because the moral law as originally given and as republished is itself a reflection of the perfections of God its author. For that reason it is binding on all people everywhere and at all times. God requires and takes pleasure in our behavior when it reflects his own righteousness. God loves in his people what he sees of himself. All men are accordingly under obligation to God their Creator and governor and to the laws of righteousness that he has given. But if all people everywhere are bound and required to honor the moral law of God by reason that they are the creatures of his hand, the more is it true that the Christian, who has been born again into the likeness of God

---

[1] Westminster Confession of Faith, XIX, 4, italics added.

himself in Christ, is bound to that law. The Christian finds in the moral law the requirements and mandates by which he structures and determines his life. The Christian loves the law of God. And though his performance of what the law requires is necessarily imperfect in this life, he nevertheless strains every nerve to obey and live in accordance with it. Certainly he does not do so because he imagines that he thereby builds favor with God. To the contrary, he does so because now he not only loves the law as it has been given, but he is compelled to obey the law by his love for God that is newly created within him. We have spoken earlier of the process of sanctification by which, though it is imperfectly developed in this life, the Christian is being conformed to the image of God's righteousness in Christ. That progressive sanctification carries with it and implies a progressive understanding of the law of righteousness itself and the Christian's desire to conform to it.

The extent to which the identity of the Christian bears on his obedience to law follows from his regeneration by which he is now joined to Christ. We may put that in the expressive terms by which the apostle described the matter to the Romans: "Where sin abounded," he said, "grace did much more abound" (Rom. 5:20). Sin abounded in Adam. When Adam sinned, we sinned. And we were bound in a state of sin by reason that Adam was our federal head and representative. The guilt of his sin was imputed to us. We were implicated in it. It was placed to our account. But Paul is here saying that when the grace of God rescued us from that state, we were raised not simply to the state that Adam enjoyed before he fell. We were raised to a much higher estate than Adam knew. Grace more abounded. The "more abounded" means that we were raised to a state of union with Christ, joined to him in an indissoluble union from which nothing can now separate us. That union contains within it the assurance that our eternal destiny and prospect are secure in Christ.

That being so, two things are to be said of the Christian

person. First, now that his or her new status in Christ is understood for what it is, it carries with it an ability to obey the law of God of which we have spoken. The Christian is no longer "dead in trespasses and sins" (Eph. 2:1). Once he was dead, but now he is alive. A dead person cannot understand the righteous law of God, let alone obey it. But now the Christian is alive and the erstwhile hatred of God and his law (Rom. 1:30) has been replaced by a love for God and his law. The grace of regeneration conveyed to him by the Holy Spirit means that he now possesses abilities and capacities of soul that were previously quite foreign to him. The Christian now has the ability by the grace of God to obey, and therefore, with a naturalness born of his newly established status in Christ, he will obey the law of God that now engages his affections.

Second, the Christian person now recognizes that the demand of obedience to God's law requires of him a spiritual discipline. "Mortify therefore your members which are upon the earth," Paul admonished the Colossian Christians (Col. 3:5). And to the same church he said, "As ye have therefore received Christ Jesus the Lord, so walk ye in him" (Col. 2:6). The scriptural data that place upon the Christian the responsibility and command to work at his or her progress in sanctification are so numerous as not to require detailed recall at this time. The meaning of what is involved was put earlier by saying that there will be no progress in sanctification unless and until there is progress in the mortification of sin. "Work out your salvation," the apostle therefore says (Phil. 2:12). Understand that you have strenuous work to do to root out the proclivities to sin that cling to old habits and imaginations. "Our old man is crucified with him [Christ], that the body of sin might be destroyed, that henceforth we should not serve sin.... Reckon ye also yourselves to be dead indeed unto sin, but alive unto God through Jesus Christ our Lord" (Rom. 6:6, 11). The motivation is there – that the Christian now has the righteousness of God in Christ clearly displayed before him.

The ability and power to obey is there – in the new strength and love for the law conveyed in the regenerating work of the Holy Spirit. And the assurance of success is there – by the fact that, as Paul continued his statement to the Philippians, "it is God which worketh in you both to will and to do of his good pleasure" (Phil. 2:13).

True religion for the Christian involves belief, obedience, and worship. The Christian life is a life that is lived in the context of worship. God, who by his faithfulness to his covenant has redeemed his people, has made it clear in his Word that he desires their worship. The Chronicler has preserved the inspired words of the Psalmist, and David has repeated their imperative, "Worship the Lord in the beauty of holiness" (1 Chr. 16:29; Ps. 29:2; 96:9). And our Lord has clarified the command that God is to be worshiped "in Spirit and in truth" (John 4:24). The Scriptural commands and mandates are clear to those who have been brought to repentance and faith in Christ by the regenerating work of the Holy Spirit. Not only is it clear that their life is to be lived "to the praise of the glory of his grace" (Eph. 1:4), and that whatever is done is to be done "to the glory of God" (1 Cor. 10:31), but they are to learn the meaning of the worship, the adoration, and the thankfulness of praise that God requires. They are to reflect upon the exalted words of the Psalmist and to rejoice with him when he says, "Enter into his gates with thanksgiving, and into his courts with praise. Be thankful to him and bless his name" (Ps. 100:4).

Throughout her long history, the church of God has wrestled with the question of proper worship. But God has always provided to his people his wishes and instructions as to how he is to be worshiped. He set forth at the beginning this commandment: "Thou shalt have no other gods before me" (Ex. 20:3). No other god, whether it be a god of things or of imagination or of activities designed for the worshiper's own pleasure, is to be admitted to the presence of the only true God. It is not to be said of the Christian, as Christ said to the

Samaritan woman, "Ye worship ye know not what" (John 4:22), or as was said of the Athenians, that they had constructed their altar "to the unknown God" (Acts 17:23). We worship the sovereign, covenant-making, redeeming and self-disclosing God who exists in infinite, eternal, and unchangeable glory, majesty, power, wisdom, holiness, and truth. We worship him for his perfections, and we return to him all thankfulness, praise, and glory for the redemption he has provided, the joy and peace of reconciliation with him, and the promise of the eternal inheritance that he has prepared for us (John 14:3; Heb. 9:15). We acknowledge his lordship in our lives. Because we have learned with the apostle to glory only "in the cross of our Lord Jesus Christ" (Gal. 6:14), we honor in our worship the Father who ordained our redemption, the Son who came into the world to accomplish our redemption, and the Holy Spirit who ministers the redeeming grace of God to us. We worship the holy, eternal, triune God. We worship God because to worship him is the highest privilege that comes within the scope and compass of our actions as his redeemed people.

The question of the proper method and content of worship has attracted varying answers in the history of the church. From the directives which God has laid down in his Word what has been referred to as "The Regulative Principle of Worship" has been deduced. That very principle, however, has been understood in different ways. On the one hand, it has been interpreted to maintain that anything that God has not expressly forbidden in his Word can be properly and legitimately included in the corporate worship activity of the church. That opens the way for the inclusion in worship of any number and kinds of human inventions that are not necessarily consistent with the demands and proprieties of God's worship "in the beauty of holiness." From that first interpretation of the Regulative Principle, therefore, the great majority of churches who hold to the Reformed theological traditions have dissented. We hold, rather, to an alternative interpretation and its consequent application of principles.

We conclude that the Word of God is precisely and securely directive, and that, as a result, only that can and should be included in the worship of the church that God has actually and positively sanctioned. We avoid, therefore, all imaginative introductions from human sources and all corresponding innovations, and we hold to what it is that the Word of God discloses as the content of corporate worship activity. That content is plainly discoverable by inspection of the inspired writings.

That includes, clearly, the reading and preaching of the Word of God, as contained in the apostolic instruction (2 Tim. 4:2), and as exhibited by apostolic practice and the expository activity of our Lord himself (Luke 4:16-21). It includes prayer, as demonstrated repeatedly in the apostolic letters, the proper administration of the sacraments, and the singing of God's praise (Matt. 26:30; Col. 3:16). Included also is the "collection for the saints" (1 Cor. 16:1) and the offerings of God's people for the work of the kingdom of Christ in this world. In such ways, it is possible to see clearly what God would have us include in the corporate worship of the church.

All that is in these ways included in corporate worship must be included because it is designed to bring honor, praise, and thankfulness to God. Worship is to be understood primarily as directed to God for his sake and for his honor. It follows that it is not a legitimate criterion of worship to include in it anything that is designed primarily for the satisfaction, in the sense of psychological or emotional fulfillment, of the individual who is purportedly worshiping. Worship is to be designed primarily to please God, not primarily to please the worshiper, though it is wonderfully true that worship to the glory of God does itself provide the greatest joy and fulfillment to the worshiper.

The Christian in the church

In what has been said of Christian worship we have anticipated an important aspect of the Christian's place in the church. The doctrine of the church requires us to bring into view from a new perspective the divine intention in redeeming a people from the estate of sin into which Adam's Fall had cast them. We have spoken in an earlier chapter of the eternal divine covenant in terms of which God designed the salvation of a particular people for himself. It is not necessary to recall at length at this point the terms of the redemption that Christ accomplished in fulfillment of that objective. "Christ loved the church and gave himself for it" (Eph. 5:25). And the church we are concerned with is "the church of God which he hath purchased with his own blood" (Acts 20:28). When we refer to the church, the first conception that occupies the mind is the church as the whole body of the elect persons whose salvation the triune God designed. We are then speaking of the church in its invisible aspect.

We distinguish the aspects of the church visible and invisible, or to employ what is common usage, the visible church and the invisible church. By the latter is meant that total body of individual persons who were the subjects of God's covenant of redemption. It includes those redeemed saints who have already departed to glory, those still to be brought to Christ by his Holy Spirit, and those numbered among God's elect who are still to be born. In their individuality and their totality they are those for whom Christ died. We do not stay further with the meaning and prospect of the Christian's inheritance as included in that great number of the elect. Our immediate concern is with the place of the Christian in the visible church, the church militant in this world as distinct from the church triumphant.

In his incorporation into the fellowship of the church the Christian is accorded the high privilege of having been transferred from the culture of the world into the distinctively new culture of the church. The two cultures are to be set in contradistinction. The Christian's status within the church is then to be viewed in terms of the blessings or privileges and the responsibilities they entail. The Christian is no longer "in the world" (Eph. 2:12). It is not possible to overemphasize the fact that the culture into which he has been incorporated in the church is distinctively different from that of the world. When we speak of the world, we refer primarily to the system of thought and belief, the thought-forms and behavior-norms, that characterize all that is antithetical to the recognition of the true God and his claims. To be "in the world" is to be captive to that godless system of belief and conduct. But the Christian is part of, and he is privileged to be a participant in, a culture that is entirely distinct from all that the world holds dear and stands for.

That elementary fact has extensive and even pervasive significance for the Christian's conduct and life. Now within the community of saints, as the apostle frequently referred to God's people (Eph. 1:1; Phil. 1:1; Col. 1:2), the Christian is the beneficiary of the means of grace that have been provided for his growth in holiness. The Spirit of God makes use of those means as he works his work of progressive sanctification. They include the hearing of God's Word preached and taught, the inclusion in the administration of the sacraments, the fellowship of God's people, and the mutual help and comfort in all exigencies that membership of the family of God provides. But beyond that, two things are to be said.

First, it is true that in God's design he calls his people to himself in Christ as individuals, with all recognition of the sanctity of their individuality and personhood. We are brought by the Spirit of God to our own individual awareness of the guilt of sin in which we stand apart from his grace, and we are each as individuals directed to the cross of Christ for the forgiveness of sin. We each bear our own individual responsibility for repentance and faith in Christ that are the instrumental cause of our salvation. But while we come into the visible church as individuals, our actions and life within the church is such that we do not behave individualistically. We recognize that we have been admitted by the grace of God to an organic entity, the entity of the church redeemed. And that in itself determines our action and conduct.

In an important respect, the church is not being progressively made up of additions to it one by one of those who are being saved. There is a sense in which, of course, that is true. But in the larger perspective we should see that the church is prior to the individual, because the church is what it is by reason of God's ordination of it before the foundation of the world. As sinners are converted and brought into the church visible the purposes of God are being realized, in that individual persons are thereby brought to the awareness of what God has ordained for them, and with respect to them, in his eternal counsel before the beginning of time.

Second, in his new position and status within the church, and with full recognition of the holy nature of the organic entity to which he has been admitted, the Christian will be careful that the culture of the church is not compromised or tarnished by importing into it the alien culture of the world. He will be careful to guard the church against the danger of capitulation to the idioms of the world, in corporate worship, language, music, and in its organization and administration. It would take us too far afield to discuss at this point the respects in which, it is to be feared, the church at large at the present time has fallen prey to such a capitulation. But we do well to consider the respects in which the preaching of the church has absorbed the philosophic thought-forms of the age, to the diminution of the true gospel of the grace of God. And we might well be alert to the respects in which the ethos of enterprise management, the pressure for entertainment that makes a travesty of the quasi-presentation of the gospel, and the clamor for cultural conformity have invaded the church. The church is in the world. And it is true, it is gravely to be feared, that the world is far too much in the church.

The Christian in the world

The distinctives of the church, as against those of the world, have been observed in brief outline in what has been said. But it remains true that the church and the Christian within the church are in the world in order that a testimony to the truth of God can be declared to all who will hear. When we contemplate the purposes of God in the redemption of his church, reflecting now on what has been said of the church in its invisible aspect, it is clear that it is by the witness and testimony of God's people that those purposes are being progressively realized and brought to consummation. That will be so until all of the elect of God have been saved. That can be put in another way. God in his immanence in the world and in his works of providence is ordering all of human history in the interests of his church. But what, then, in the light of that, is to be the nature of the Christian's conduct and testimony?

In short, two principal conclusions follow. First, the Christian is to live, with all the scrupulosity that by the grace of God he commands, in such a way that it is clear that he now belongs to Christ. He is a new person by the redeeming grace of God and he is to live before the world in such a way that the implications of that newness of personhood are apparent. There are, in every aspect of life and its commitments, in its work, sciences, and entertainments, two kinds of people. There are those who have been made regenerate by the grace of God, and there are those who are still in the unregenerate state of sinful commitments and orientation. That there are two kinds of people implies two radically different kinds of commitments, activities, goals, and orientations. The Christian, to employ the scriptural admonition at this point, is to be the salt and the light that bring to the world both the conviction of its sin on the one hand and the possibility of relief in the love of Christ on the other.

Second, in discharging that important obligation the Christian will inevitably attract the opprobrium and even the persecution of the world. There is no point in rejecting that inevitability and necessity. Our Lord himself has made the point clear. "The servant is not greater than his lord. If they have persecuted me, they will also persecute you" (John 15:20). Again the relevant Scripture could be multiplied. But it is equally relevant to say that the Scriptures contain clear guidance as to how the Christian should walk in and before the world. "Walk in wisdom toward them that are without," Paul said to the Colossians. "Let your speech be alway with grace, seasoned with salt, that ye may know how ye ought to answer every man" (Col. 4:5-6). "Walk honestly toward them that are without" (1 Thes. 4:12). The Christian will be careful that his life and conduct speak clearly of the mercy and grace of God, with a love for the souls of men and a wish that they might be saved.

In the Christian's well-intentioned wish to be faithful to that obligation he will avoid a twofold danger that may tarnish his testimony. First, he will avoid the damaging tendency to be silent when he should have spoken. That is all too present a danger, meaning that one may be willing in many situations and circumstances to take what appears to be an easy way out simply by being silent, saying nothing, and by default conforming to habits and activities that characterize the world rather than the kingdom of Christ. Second, the danger exists at the other extreme that the Christian will act injudiciously and speak when he should be silent. That possibility arises when an over-enthusiastic Christian tarnishes his testimony to the truth of God by unnecessary brow-beating his or her associates at work or in other permissible and legitimate situations. It is pertinent to remember that our Lord said: "Blessed are ye when men shall revile you, and persecute you, and shall say all manner of evil against you falsely, for my sake" (Matt. 5:11). But he said that the persecution he had in view was "for my sake." The Christian does well to be sure that the persecution that may come is for Christ's sake, and not for the sake of, or because of, the Christian's own injudicious actions and behavior. It is an important truth that frequently the testimony that God would have us give is to be seen in the manner of life we live before the world, and which those with whom we necessarily associate in the routine functions of life observe us to live.

Conclusion

From our review of Christian doctrine and its meaning for the life and walk of faith two conclusions follow. First, and taking account of the state of sin in which we existed by reason of Adam's Fall, God is sovereign in the sinner's salvation. God is sovereign in all parts of salvation, in the sinner's regeneration, justification, and sanctification. Second, the new-born person, now joined to Christ in an indissoluble union, will pursue with a new naturalness the holiness and righteousness of life that speaks consistency with the law of God.

Those conclusions call for only brief comment at this stage. God's sovereignty in salvation is to be considered in several respects. By it we mean that the sinner plays no meritorious part in his salvation. We have seen that because of the Fall the faculties of the soul are disabled as to the possibility of any action of eternal value. The mind of the natural man is darkened and cannot know or understand the things of God (1 Cor. 2:14). The heart is perverse and altogether turned to hate God (Rom. 1:30). And as a result the will is bound and no longer free to move in obedience to God and his law. Such is the sorry state of man in sin. It is clear that man cannot save himself. If he could in his natural state do anything of eternal or spiritual value, and if, as a result, his salvation turned on his own contribution to it, he would in effect be sovereignly responsible for his own salvation. Salvation would then be an autosoterism. If it were said that the sinner in his disabled state nevertheless possessed abilities to cooperate with the grace of God in salvation, then salvation would be a synergism, a jointly determined outcome, partly the work of man and partly the work of the grace of God. But our doctrine is that salvation is not an autosoterism, nor is it a synergism. Salvation is a divine monergism. It is due solely to the sovereign, unsolicited wakening within the soul of the new life that the Spirit of God imparts. That, it is now being said, means that God is sovereign in the sinner's regeneration. The new life born in the soul is altogether the sovereign work of God.

We may recall the manner in which our Puritan forefathers spoke of the same condition and outcome. It was usual in the seventeenth century to speak of what we have termed regeneration under the heading of the Holy Spirit's effectual calling. In that connection it was said, "Effectual calling is the work of God's Spirit, whereby, convincing us of our sin and misery, enlightening our minds in the knowledge of Christ, and renewing our wills, he doth persuade and enable us to embrace Jesus Christ, freely offered to us in the gospel."[2] The sovereignty of God in that remarkable transformation of the sinner is thus clearly displayed.

When it is said that God is sovereign in the sinner's justification it is recalled that the justification of the sinner turns on what we have seen as the declarative, forensic, once-for-all statement by God that the righteousness of Christ has been imputed to the sinner, or placed to his account. That follows, it has equally clearly been seen, on the sinner's exercise of repentance for sin and faith and trust in Christ. But the sovereignty of God in the sinner's justification is displayed in the fact that faith and repentance are themselves the gift of God. The repentant sinner is turned to Christ only because the Spirit of God has imparted to him the gift of faith that Christ purchased for him in his atoning work. Now that the soul is renewed by the new life that God's gracious act of regeneration imparts, the person, now alive and no longer dead in sin, is able to act and turn to God in Christ. That action is, of

---

[2] Westminster Shorter Catechism, Question 31.

course, the action of the person himself. But our doctrine maintains clearly that the sinner in his turning to Christ does not make any *meritorious* action in doing so. We have put that previously by stating that the *efficient* cause of salvation is the grace of God. "By grace are ye saved" (Eph. 2:8). The *meritorious* cause is the atoning work of Christ. And the *instrumental* cause is the sinner's faith, now communicated to him by the Spirit of God.

When we say that God is sovereign in all parts of salvation it follows that God is sovereign also in the Christian's sanctification. We have looked at an earlier stage at the process of sanctification and the work of the Spirit of God in it. We have seen the heavy responsibility laid upon the Christian to pursue the means of grace that God has provided for his progress in holiness. At this concluding point it is sufficient to say that sanctification is the sovereign work of God because every motivation to it is the gift of God in fulfillment of the statement of the apostle that God has made Christ to be to the sinner whom he has redeemed "wisdom and righteousness and sanctification and redemption" (1 Cor. 1:30). We have seen also the meaning of the discipline that the Spirit of God exercises in the lives of his people to bring them to the condition of holiness that he has ordained for them (Heb. 12:6-7). The motivation to holiness, the desire after holiness, and the power and ability to pursue holiness are all the work of the sovereign Spirit of God in the soul.

Our final conclusion follows from what has now been said. It is that beside and because of the sovereignty of God in salvation, the Christian will pursue the means of progress in holiness in life and righteousness in conduct with a new naturalness. It is that new naturalness of disposition in pursuit of the things of God that marks the new-born person who now enjoys an ineradicable place in the family of God. He or she is now adopted into, and has a right to all the privileges of, the family of God. Now by the perfect work of Christ, his sinless life in fulfillment of the law of God and his substitutionary death in payment of the penalty for the broken law, the Christian's status is secure in his redemption for time and for all eternity.

Well has the apostle exclaimed, "Thanks be unto God for his unspeakable gift" (2 Cor. 9:15). May we who belong to him join in the praise and the eternal worship due him for his gracious gift at no less a price than the giving of his own Son for our redemption.

Index of Scripture References

Genesis
1:28	71, 139
1:31	86
2:7	87
2:19-20	140
3:8	86, 90, 139, 173
3:21	75
6:5	92
9:6	89
14:18	80
17:9	79
50:20	42

Exodus
20:3	178

Deuteronomy
6:4	34

Joshua
2:3	80
21:43-45	77

Ruth
1:16	80

1 Kings
8:27	59

1 Chronicles
16:29	178

2 Chronicles
2:6	59

Psalms
5:5	98
19:1	24
19:12	152
29:2	178
33:11	65
51:5	99
89:35	39
96:9	178
100:4	178
103:12	137
116:3	134
139:7-10	60

Song of Solomon
3:1	160

Isaiah
1:14	98
6:3	38
53:4-6	126
53:10-12	126
61:1	54
63:10	98
66:1	60

Jeremiah
17:9	93

23:24	60	**Mark**	
24:7	53	10:45	36
31:31	81, 123		
31:33	123	**Luke**	
44:4	98	2:14	48
		4:16-21	54, 180
Ezekiel		9:51	134
16:43	98	10:22	32
		11:19-22	93
Daniel		11:21-22	14
9:27	125		
		John	
Hosea		1:1	109
6:3	53	1:11	15
		1:14	109
Amos		1:18	25, 81
3:6	42	1:29	81, 135, 174
4:2	39	3:3	29
		3:15	82
Micah		3:16	36, 124
5:2	54	4:7	80
		4:22	179
Habakkuk		4:24	178
3:13	98	5:39	54, 57, 126
		6:37	16, 32
Zechariah		6:44	17, 162
8:17	98	6:45	17
		8:33-34	93
Malachi		10:3	11
2:8	125	10:11	11
2:10	125	10:14	11
3:1	125	10:15	11, 131
4:2	125	10:28	11
		10:30	32
Matthew		10:32-33	13
1:21	125, 131, 138	10:34	14
5:11	185	14:2-3	172
15:22-28	80	14:3	179
26:30	180	14:8-9	32
28:19	33	14:9	25

Index of Scripture References

14:26	32	8:1	163
15:18-19	15	8:13	168
15:20	185	8:28	62
16:8	32	8:29	66
16:13	32, 53	9:17	42
16:13-14	68		
16:14	32	**1 Corinthians**	
16:16	32	1:18	122
17:3	9, 21	1:30	31, 119, 166, 188
17:6	11, 67, 128	2:14	29, 92, 186
17:9	67	10:13	158
17:11	67	10:31	178
17:17	168	13:12	109
21:25	51	15:22	5
		16:1	180
Acts			
1:11	120, 136	**2 Corinthians**	
2:23	66	4:4	57, 92
4:28	66	4:6	57, 92
15:18	61	5:17	148
16:14	162	5:21	163
17:23	179	9:15	82, 189
17:28	23		
20:27	65	**Galatians**	
20:28	11, 181	2:20	157
		3:13	78, 80
Romans		3:14	80
1:18	23	3:17	76
1:18-20	22	3:29	76
1:30	23, 95, 148, 177, 186	6:14	179
3:10	79, 99		
3:23	79, 99	**Ephesians**	
3:26	163	1:1	152, 182
4:11	78	1:3-4	73
5:12	5, 71, 99	1:4	66, 178
5:19	5, 36, 133, 164	1:4-5	124
5:20	176	1:10	172
6:6	177	1:11	62, 65, 66
6:11	177	2:1	144, 162, 177
6:16	94	2:5-6	144
6:17	94	2:8	119, 163, 188

2:12	14, 182	**2 Timothy**	
4:5-6	185	2:11	41
4:13	10, 30	3:16	47
4:24	40, 104	4:2	17, 180
4:30	157		
5:24	11	**Titus**	
5:25	131, 181	3:5	37
Philippians		**Hebrews**	
1:1	152, 182	1:1-2	25
1:6	167	1:2	11, 143
2:7-8	114	1:3	117, 137, 174
2:12	167, 177	1:13	98
2:13	31, 178	2:10	117
		2:14	14
Colossians		2:18	117, 135
1:2	152, 182	4:14	76
1:12-13	151	4:14-16	117
1:13	14, 119	4:15	135
1:17	42	5:8-9	117
2:3	141	6:17	77
2:6	177	7:25	81
3:4	10	7:27	134
3:5	177	8:7-13	81
3:10	104	9:11-12	137
3:16	180	9:12	134
4:5-6	185	9:15	11, 143, 179
		9:24	138
1 Thessalonians		9:26	134
4:3	163	9:28	134
4:12	185	10:4	137
		10:16	123
1 Timothy		10:16-17	81
1:15	106	10:17	137
1:17	59	11:31	80
3:16	108	12:6-7	188
6:15-16	59	12:14	10, 167
6:16	38, 85		

James
1:14	154
3:9	89

1 Peter
1:2	66, 124
1:18-20	135
2:9	151
2:24	135
3:18	55, 134

2 Peter
1:3-4	3
1:10	167
1:21	47
3:11	37, 172
3:16	55

1 John
1:5-7	106
2:15-17	15
3:2	10, 120
3:4	97
3:6	156
3:8	14
3:9	156, 157
4:2	109
4:10	32, 124
5:6-7	106

Revelation
3:20	169
4:8	38
5:10	142

Index of Subjects and Names

Abrams, M., 2
Adultery, 125, 175
Agnosticism, 34
Alexander, A., 2
Alexander, C., 107
Alexander J., 62
Animals, 140
Anthropology, 83
Antitype, 64, 80, 136, 174
Aquinas, T., 8
Arius, 112
Ark of the covenant, 136, 174
Arminius, 108
Arminianism, 108, 120
Athanasius, 33, 112
Atheism, 1, 22
Atonement, 16, 75, 109, 118,
  Day of, 80, 136
  extent of, 128
  indiscriminate, 16
  limited, 131,
  necessity of, 126-27
    absolute, 127
    hypothetical, 127
  particular, 16, 130-31
  universal, 130-32
  substitutionary, 79, 166
Augustine, 69
Authority, 4, 85
Autonomy, 1, 71, 102, 171
  assertion of, 102-03, 139
  epistemological, 102-03
  ethical, 102-03
  metaphysical, 102
Autosoterism, 186-87

Baptism, 79
Barrenness of soul, 159
Bavinck, H., 2
Becoming, 61
Being, 61
Belief, 171-72
Benediction, 19, 24, 78
  see also Malediction
Berkhof, L., 2, 65, 66, 116
Bondage, 13, 93
  of the will, 93

Calling, 62
  see also effectual calling
Calvin, J., 2, 24
Capital punishment, 89
Categories
  of explanation, 140
  of interpretation, 46
Chain of being, 95
Chalmers, T., 2
Chance, 141
Charnock, S., 38, 98, 99
Chastisement, 168
Christ
  bread of life, 162
  communication of
    properties in, 111
  cry of dereliction of, 116
  divine attributes of, 114
  divine identity, 114
  divine nature of, 52, 72
  divine Person, 110, 135
  glory of, 114
  high priesthood of, 76, 81,

117, 121-22, 134-35, 137
  heavenly priesthood, 81,
    123, 135, 138
    intercession in, 138
    sympathy in, 138
  human nature of, 52, 67,
    72, 107, 109-10, 136
  human soul, 110
  impeccability of, 115
  incarnation of, 72, 107,
    108, 109, 111, 117, 136
  messenger of the covenant,
    125
  obedience of, 36, 107, 117,
    122-3, 132
    active, 117, 133
    passive, 117, 133
    substitutionary, 162
  Person of, 109-10
    theanthropic, 110
  pre-existence of, 33
  redemptive office of, 67,
    125, 138
    king, 138-39, 142
    prophet, 138-39, 142
    priest, 138-39
  righteousness of, 100, 163
  satisfaction of, 123
  self-existence of, 33-34
  sinlessness of, 109
  soul of, 117
  substitute, 67, 70, 72, 79,
    133-34, 139-40
  substitutionary sacrifice of,
    36, 98, 108, 123
  unipersonality of, 115
Christ-event, 124, 135
Christological settlement,
  113
Church, 12, 142, 149, 152,
  154, 160, 166, 172
  culture of, 13, 15, 17
  doctrine of, 10, 12
  government of, 12
  invisible aspect, 12, 181
  militant, 12
  organic entity of, 183
  triumphant, 12, 181
  visible aspect of, 12, 181
  worship of, 12
Circumcision, 79, 174
Commingling of eternal and
  temporal, 118, 120
Common grace, 74, 75, 92,
  105, 141, 142
  negative aspect of, 74
  positive aspect of, 74
Concupiscence, 154
Conscience, 68
Consubstantiation, 112
Contrary habitual principle,
  155
Council
  of Chalcedon, 113
  of Nicea, 112
  of Trent, 154
Council of redemption, 65
Covenant, 178
  Abrahamic, 77
  new, 64, 75, 76, 81, 123
  of common grace, 64, 74
  of creation, 19, 64
    parties of, 70
  of grace, 64, 71-73, 84,
    122-23, 129
    forms of administration
      of, 73, 75, 76
    parties of, 73
    subjects of, 128, 129
  of redemption, 58, 64, 65,
    70, 72, 73, 123, 128
    parties of, 67

Index of Subjects and Names

subjects of, 129
of works, 64, 71
unfulfilled requirements of, 72
theology, 57
Covenantal administration, 64
Covenantal obligations, 5, 18, 23, 78, 85, 102, 125
repudiation of, 102, 145
Covenantal promise, 167
Covenantal redemption, 167
Covenantal theology, 19, 57, 63
Cowper, W., 159
Creation mandate, 104
Creation ordinances, 50
Creator-creature distinction, 96
Creaturehood, 102
Cultural accommodation, 1
Culture, 6, 17, 74, 92, 161, 170-71
of the church, 13, 15, 17, 161, 182
of the world, 14, 181
Cunningham, W., 2, 154
Curse, 24, 126

Dabney, R., 2, 146, 150, 153-54
Davie, D., 159
Day of Atonement, 80, 136
Dereliction, 116
Discipline, 161
Disobedience, 36, 78
Divinization, 29
Docetism, 111
Doctrine, 3
Dogma, 3
Donum superadditum, 86

Edwards, J., 2, 90
Effectual calling, 17, 37, 62, 145
Elect, 66
Election, 69, 70, 167
Enlightenment, 8
Epistemology, 102
Eschatological person, 172
Eternal security, 69

Facts, 46, 61
brute, 46
preinterpretation of, 46
reinterpretation of, 46
uninterpreted, 46
Faculties of the soul, 56, 83, 87, 90, 92, 94, 95, 104, 132
effect of regeneration on, 145, 148
effect of sin on, 87, 91, 92
effect of the fall on, 186
emotional, 89, 91, 94
harmony of, 90, 91, 104
intellectual, 89, 90
judicial, 89
prince of faculties, 90, 91, 104
volitional, 89
Faculty psychology, 90
Faith, 12, 68, 119, 160, 182, 186-87
persevering, 165
obedient, 165
Fall, 5, 8, 23, 49, 63, 69, 84, 128, 131, 139, 186
an ethical lapse, 95, 97
Federal head, 44, 70, 100, 101
Finitude, 26, 44, 120

Glorification, 62

Gnosticism, 111
God, 21
  attributes of, 27, 28, 31, 38, 51, 60, 113
    communicable, 28
    incommunicable, 28, 42
  counsel of, 65, 66
  covenant-keeping, 63
  covenant-making, 24, 63,
  decrees of, 12, 68
  essence of, 27, 28, 33, 34, 39, 40, 43, 51
  eternity of, 29, 179
  face of, 158
  foreknowledge of, 66, 113
  foreordination of, 113
  glory of, 37, 41
  grace of, 24, 29, 43, 81, 119
  holiness of, 37, 39-41, 113
  honor of, 71, 122
  immanence of, 41, 42, 107, 184
  immensity of, 59
  immortality of, 38, 58, 59
  immutability of, 29
  infinity of, 29, 42, 179
  justice of, 24, 39, 71, 122, 123, 163
  knowledge of, 58, 113
  law of, 40, 123, 133
  love of, 39
  majesty of, 37
  mercy of, 23, 98
  oath of, 77
  omnipotence of, 60
  omnipresence of, 42, 60
  omniscience of, 60
  personal, 24
  proofs of, 8, 9, 22
  purposeful, 24
  purposes of, 51
  redemptive offices of, 9, 35, 67, 123, 129
  righteousness of, 39-41, 164
  self-disclosure of, 25
  self-existence of, 40
  sovereignty of, 30, 37, 119, 168, 186-88
  transcendence of, 38, 40, 41
  truthfulness of, 39
  will of
    decretive, 167
    preceptive, 167
  wrath of, 39, 97, 123
Godhead
  attributes of, 118
  being of Persons, 130
  consubstantiality of Persons, 31
  council of, 124
  eternal generation of the Son, 34
  intratrinitarian communication in, 66
  knowledge of Persons, 129
  names of Persons, 33
  simplicity of, 35
  trinity of Persons, 31-33, 35, 179
  unity of, 33, 34, 35
  works of Persons, 129
Goodwin, T., 2
Grace, 23
Graham, B., 131
Gray, T., 141
Gregory, 35
Guilt, 71, 81, 130, 176
  ceremonial, 81, 137

Habitus, 150, 153, 154
Hermeneutical principle, 57

High priest, 80, 134, 174
Hodge, A., 42, 43, 111
Hodge, C., 2
Holiness, 10, 26, 37, 156,
  166, 172, 182, 186, 188
  ceremonial, 80, 137
Holy Spirit
  effectual call of, 145
  internal testimony of, 55-57
  redemptive office of, 67,
   145
Hope, 13
Howe, J., 2

Image of God, See Man
Impeccability, 115
Imputation, 5, 83, 94, 99,
  100, 163-64
  immediate, 100, 101
  mediate, 100, 101
  of Adam's sin, 99-101, 176
  of Christ's righteousness,
   100
Incarnation
  See Christ, incarnation of
Individuality, 160
Indwelling sin
  see Sin, indwelling
Integral personhood
  see Man, personhood
Internal testimony of the
  Spirit, 55-57
Intratrinitarian
  communication, 66

Justification, 10, 62, 161,
  162, 165
  declarative, 161-62
  forensic, 161, 163, 187
  ground of, 10, 162

Kant, I., 8, 108
Kenotic theory, 114
Knowledge
  analogical, 28
  of God, 21, 28, 51, 52, 91

Language, 52
Law, 50
  God-created, 141
  of God, 40, 123, 133, 171
   ceremonial, 50, 173-75
   civil, 50, 173-75
   judicial, 50, 173
   moral, 50, 173-75
   rule of life, 51
  of logic, 88
  transgression of, 99
Levitical priesthood, 80
Logic, 88
Lust, 154
Lutheran theology, 111, 112

Machen, G., 2
Malediction, 19, 24, 78, 79,
  126
  see also Benediction
Man
  a covenantal creature, 85
  analogue of God, 85, 87, 96
  assumption of autonomy of,
   75
  awareness of God, 23
  bodily aspect, 156
  covenantal obligations of,
   5, 85
  derivative authority of, 85
  derivative holiness of, 85,
   86, 102
  derivative immortality of,
   85, 87

derivative knowledge, 102
derivative personhood of, 85, 170
fall of, 5, 86
  see also Fall
God-consciousness of, 23
image of God, 4, 24, 25, 83, 84, 87-89, 95, 146, 170
immortal, 87
moral, 88
nature of
  new, 147, 149
  old, 147, 149
  regenerate, 145, 147
  sinful, 145, 149
original holiness, 26, 86, 91
original offices,
  king, 70, 71, 85, 139
  priest, 70, 71, 85, 139
  prophet, 70, 71, 85, 139
original righteousness, 26
perfectibility of, 83
personality of, 146, 150, 151
personhood of, 6, 147, 182
  integral, 147-49, 153
probation of, 19, 26, 90
rational, 87
self-awareness of, 27
self-consciousness of, 5, 85
soul, 146
spiritual, 87
Marriage, 51, 173
Materialism, 1
Means of grace, 160, 167-8
Melchisedek, 80
Mercy, 23, 136
Mercy seat, 80, 136
Milton, J., 2
Modernism, 1
Monergism, 187

Mortification, 168, 177
Mosaic administration, 79, 80, 123, 136-37, 173
Murray, J., 2, 8, 127, 146, 151, 155, 165
Mystery, 34, 43, 108, 118

Newman, J., 107
Noumenal realm, 9

Oath, 77
Obedience, 23, 36, 71, 78, 172-73, 176
opera ad intra 34, 65
orthography, 48
  see also Scripture
Owen, J., 2, 154, 155, 157, 158, 159

Packer, J., 45
Paradise, 71
Paradox, 147, 151
Passover, 174
Pelagius, 69, 131
Perdition, 97
Persecution, 185
Perseverance, 68
Personhood, 6, 7
Plymouth Brethren, 149
Post-Christian age, 7
Postmodernism, 1
Prayer, 160
Predestination, 62, 69
Presuppositions, 1, 9, 22, 88
Probability, 61
Probation, 19, 26, 71, 90
Proofs of God, 8, 9, 22
  cosmological, 8
  moral, 8
  ontological, 8
  teleological, 8

Prophecy, 54
Propitiation, 98, 124
Providence, 42, 64, 120, 184

Randomness, 141
Ransom, 36
Reconciliation, 70
Redemption, 10, 16, 23, 36, 70, 106, 108, 124, 142
  benefits of, 19
  Christological interpretation of, 19
  design of, 36
  state of, 23
Regeneration, 30, 37, 119, 132, 144, 145, 147-48, 150, 165, 177, 186-87
Religion, 4, 6
Repentance, 12, 68, 162, 182,
Revelation 6, 22, 50
  anthropomorphic, 52, 65
  authoritative, 25
  necessity of, 26
  partial, 51, 52, 90, 91
Reymond, R., 2
Righteousness, 26, 37, 40,
  constitutive, 164
  forensic, 163
Rule of life, 51
  See also law of God

Sabbath, 51, 173
Sabellianism, 33, 112
Sacraments, 161, 180, 182
Salvation
  efficient cause, 162, 188
  instrumental cause, 163, 182, 188
  meritorious cause, 163, 188
  sovereignty of God in, 186
Sanctification, 10, 31, 53, 124, 145, 148, 150, 161, 165, 177, 182, 188
  definitive, 165
  progressive, 30, 166, 176
  sovereignty of God in, 168
Schaff, P., 112
Scofield Bible, 149
Scougal, H., 157
Scripture, 44, 53, 54
  authoritative, 45, 48
  authority of, 49, 50
  autographs of, 47, 48
  criterion of truth, 44
  human authorship of, 47
  inerrant, 45
  infallible, 45
  inspiration of, 45-47
  key to, 57
  necessity of, 26, 49, 50
  orthography in, 48
  paraphrase of, 47
  perspicuity of, 49
  preservation of, 48
  self-authentication, 56
  sufficiency of, 49, 50
  translation of, 47
Semen religionis, 26
Sensus deitatis, 26
Shedd, W., 116
Sin, 14, 19, 26, 50, 70, 94
  assertion of autonomy, 102, 103
  covenantal repudiation, 102, 145
  depravation of, 96
  deprivation of, 96
  ethical lapse, 95, 97
  guilt of, 71, 99
  imputation of, 83, 94, 100
  indwelling, 147, 155
  secret, 152

self-direction of, 94, 104-5
state of, 97, 132
transgression of law, 97
Sinful nature, 145, 149
Smeaton, G., 2, 35
Social relations, 51
Solidarity, 160
Sproul, R., 164
Subordination, 35
Sun of Righteousness, 125
Synergism, 186, 187

Ten Commandments, 50-51, 174-75
Theology, 6, 171
covenant, 57, 63
Thornwell, J., 2
Time, 52, 58-60, 69, 107, 113, 118, 120, 134
Transubstantiation, 112
Tree of life, 24, 78, 96
Trinity, consubstantiality, 31
Trinity, 35, 36
economic, 35
ontological, 35
see also Godhead
Turretin, F., 2, 24, 25, 28, 30, 34, 163
Two natures theory, 15, 149, 150-51

Union with Christ, 11, 12, 30, 143, 156, 165, 169, 173, 176, 186

Van Til, C., 2, 45
Venning, R., 152, 153
Verbal inspiration, 46
see also Scripture
Vicegerent, 139
Vickers, D., 33, 45, 63, 69, 84, 90, 112
Vos, G., 2

Warfield, B., 2, 45
Watershed of history, 122
Weeks, N., 45
Wesley, C., 108
Wesley, J., 131
Will, 93, 94
bondage of, 93
of God
decretive, 167
preceptive, 167
Witsius, H., 2, 63
Work, 51, 173
Worship, 51, 172-73, 178-79
corporate, 180
regulative principle of, 179

Young, E., 45

www.ingramcontent.com/pod-product-compliance
Lightning Source LLC
Chambersburg PA
CBHW030319080526
44584CB00012B/621